AF621678

100% UNOFFICIAL

100% UNOFFICIAL

100% UNOFFICIAL

100% UNOFFICIAL

100% UNOFFICIAL

100% UNOFFICIAL

First published in Great Britain 2026 by 100% Unofficial, a part of Farshore
An imprint of Harper*CollinsPublishers*
1 London Bridge Street, London SE1 9GF
www.farshore.co.uk

Harper*CollinsPublishers*
Macken House, 39/40 Mayor Street Upper,
Dublin 1, D01 C9W8, Ireland

Written by Malcolm Croft

This book is an original creation by Farshore

ISBN 978 0 00 879451 4
Printed in Romania
001

A CIP catalogue record for this title is available from the British Library.

100% UNOFFICIAL

BTS ANNUAL 2027

CONTENTS

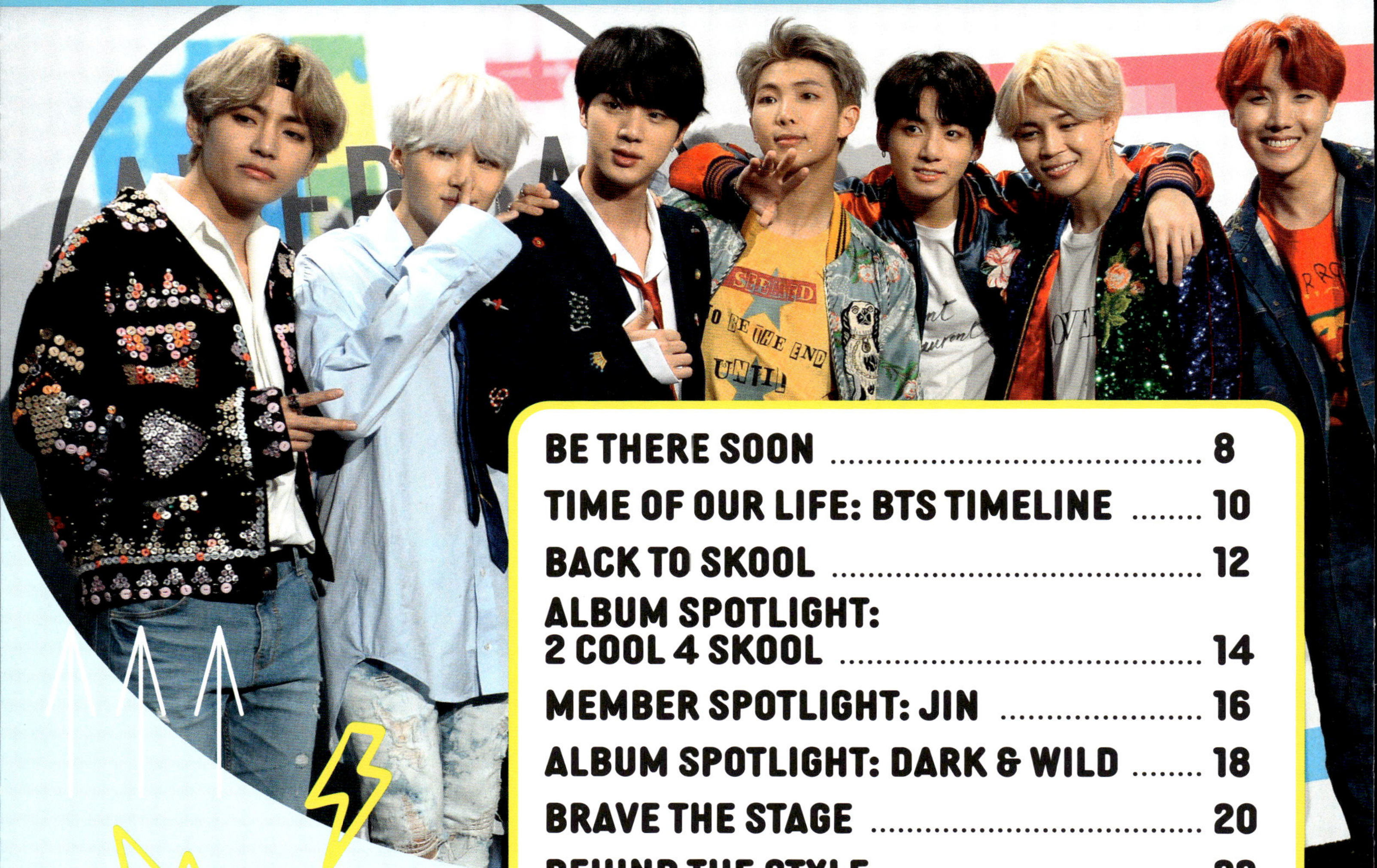

BE THERE SOON 8
TIME OF OUR LIFE: BTS TIMELINE 10
BACK TO SKOOL 12
ALBUM SPOTLIGHT: 2 COOL 4 SKOOL 14
MEMBER SPOTLIGHT: JIN 16
ALBUM SPOTLIGHT: DARK & WILD 18
BRAVE THE STAGE 20
BEHIND THE STYLE 22
MEMBER SPOTLIGHT: SUGA 24
ALBUM SPOTLIGHT: THE MOST BEAUTIFUL MOMENT IN LIFE, PT. 1 26
BEHOLD THE SCREAMS! 28
ALBUM SPOTLIGHT: WINGS 30
MEMBER SPOTLIGHT: J-HOPE 32
BETWEEN THE SCREENS 34
BORN TO SING! 36
BREAK THE STATES! 38

40

MEMBER SPOTLIGHT: RM 40
ALBUM SPOTLIGHT: LOVE YOURSELF: TEAR 42
BREAK THE SWEAT! 44
BEGIN THE SHOWS! 46
MEMBER SPOTLIGHT: JIMIN 48
ALBUM SPOTLIGHT: MAP OF THE SOUL: 7 50
BEYOND THE STUDIO 52
BRIDGE THE SOUNDS 54
MEMBER SPOTLIGHT: V 56
ALBUM SPOTLIGHT: BE 58
BEYOND THE STARS 60
BIG TIME SUCCESS 62
MEMBER SPOTLIGHT: JUNGKOOK 64
BILLION TOTAL STREAMS 66
BE THE SPARK 68

64

60

BE THERE SOON

The boys are back! In 2026, BTS returned after three years – bolder, bigger and better than ever before. Are YOU ready?

Where BTS belong – on a stage for all of us to see!

IN THE ARMY NOW

On 17th October, 2022, BTS announced they were taking a hiatus, their first in ten years. It was for good reason: they enlisted into the South Korean Military, mandatory for all South Korean men under 30. Jin, the oldest member, was the first to enlist. Suga was last. His service ended in June 2025. The group staggered their service so that all seven members were unavailable for no more than six months.

RM and V say goodbye to the military.

THE WAIT IS OVER!

A date that will live in musical infamy – 1st July, 2025 – was the day that BTS announced they were returning to active band duties! The news made world headlines and amassed hundreds of millions of social media posts. It was Jimin (naturally!) who first broke the news of the band's reunion and RM told the ARMY the news everyone wanted to hear: "All seven of us will begin working closely together on new music!"

RM dripping in swag at Milan's Fashion Week, Sept 2025.

HYBE announce BTS's return – so cool!

"HEY GUYS, WE'RE BACK!"

Together, in person, for the first time in nearly four years, BTS's smiles were beamed around the world via their 30-minute WeVerse livestream broadcast. The band, sat around together laughing, amassed more than seven million real-time views, a record for the WeVerse platform.

"I look forward to when our members will have completed their service. We will get together and talk about what BTS can do in the future. I think it's going to be a massive energy!"
J-Hope, speaking in 2025 after completing his military service.

ALL AROUND THE WORLD

Also announced in their reunion WeVerse chat was news of a brand new world tour – a massive 82-date jaunt from April 2026 to March 2027, covering 34 cities across 23 countries, spanning five continents! "We'll be visiting fans all around the world," the band said proudly. "We hope you're as excited as we are!" Did you get a ticket?

ARIRANG!

Completed in November 2025, according to Jimin, *Arirang's* title sparked worldwide headlines, with millions of international ARMY members speculating about what on earth it meant. The word dates back to its first recorded use in 1756, naming a beloved folk song that has been sung for generations and one that stands as a symbol of unity between South and North Korea. Deeply meaningful to all Koreans, *Arirang* has also been described as a battle cry meaning 'my beloved one', representing a hazardous journey filled with hope.

A KIND OF BEAUTY

Ahead of *Arirang's* release in 2026 RM reassured ARMY that he was "working diligently" in "faraway Los Angeles" and that the project already felt "weird". He shared that the group had returned to routine: wake up at ten, workouts, breakfast and creative work until nine at night. Reflecting on the process, RM said: "Making something together with these friends, I'm going to commit myself to this moment. I hope that it will be a kind of beauty." We weren't disappointed!

Looking dapper at the United Nations in NYC.

BTS MOVIE WEEKS

A global cinema event celebrating the band's legacy ahead of their 2026 comeback, BTS Movie Weeks were screened at cinemas, featuring concert films such as *Burn the Stage*, *Bring the Soul* and *Yet to Come in Cinemas*. The Movie Weeks united ARMY worldwide to relive BTS's greatest moments, ahead of their long-awaited return.

BACK TO THE START

On 20th March, 2026, the group released their tenth album, *Arirang*, the band's fifth studio recording since *BE* in 2022. On release, it broke the record for 'most-streamed album in a single day in 2026 so far', and also set a new record as the 'most-streamed K-Pop album in Spotify history'. "We're planning to make something massive!" RM said when the new album was revealed on WeVerse in July 2025. "We're approaching it with the same mindset we had when we first started."

ARIRANG TRACK LIST

1. Body to Body
2. Hooligan
3. Aliens
4. FYA
5. 2.0
6. No. 29
7. SWIM
8. Merry Go Round
9. NORMAL
10. Like Animals
11. they don't know 'bout us
12. One More Night
13. Please
14. Into The Sun

TIME OF OUR LIFE: BTS TIMELINE

BTS has enjoyed so many amazing moments on their incredible rise to worldwide fame. These early milestones hit the hardest ...

2010

30TH SEPTEMBER

Do you remember this day? If you're ARMY, you do! It was one of the earliest times the name 'Bulletproof Boy Scouts' appeared, in the pre-debut track **'Asurada'** (or **'Ashes'**), a collaboration between RM, Iron and Supreme Boi. In Korean, Bulletproof Boy Scouts is pronounced *Bangtan Sonyeondan* and written as 방탄소년단.

2012

7TH DECEMBER

That day marks the moment BTS first introduced themselves on Twitter (now X). Their debut tweet was:

"Wassup! We're BTS. Finally, the BTS Twitter account is officially open – Clap clap clap! We will be uploading fun things beyond your imagination here until our debut."

A few days later, on 23rd December, Jin gifted the world the very first BTS selfie, showing off his trademark pouty lower lip. In 2017, the group become the most tweeted-about artists of all time and today BTS are the most popular band on X, with more than 48 million followers!

2013

13TH JUNE

D-day! Debut day! It was on this awesome day that the group made their stage debut on *M Countdown*, a weekly South Korean music TV show, with the single **'No More Dream'**. Unbelievably, the song was not successful upon the group's debut, debuting at No.84 in the top 100 in Korea. However, the song did finally reach the No.1 spot on the Billboard World Digital Song Sales chart in December 2023 – a decade after its release!

2013

9TH JULY

Now celebrated each year as ARMY Day, 9th July marks the moment BTS revealed the official name for their fandom – ARMY! From this date forward, fans weren't just fans, they were a global cultural movement, the largest of its kind. You're a member of ARMY, aren't you?

"So many miracles have happened to us! But we're just getting started. There are still more amazing things to accomplish for BTS."

RM, feeling reflective on the band's meteoric rise to fame.

The K-Pop Awards 2015 – their first major award win!

2013

14TH NOVEMBER

The day – just five months after their debut – BTS were recognised as Best New Artist of the Year at the Melon Music Awards in Seoul, South Korea – their first ever major award win! It was a win that opened the doors for BTS to collect numerous other awards in 2014, often for 'Rookies of the Year'.

2019

Spot the odd one out – Jimin as usual!

13TH APRIL

BTS becoming big stars in the United States is much more important than you might think. It truly showed that their music was universal. When the group walked out onstage as the first ever K-Pop group to perform on New York's *Saturday Night Live*, America's iconic TV show, it became the most talked about moment of the year. The episode introduced BTS to more than ten million US viewers as they performed **'Boy With Luv'**.

How do you celebrate Suga Day?

BTS BIRTHDAYS - DON'T FORGET!

1. **Jin** – 4th December, 1992
2. **Suga** – 9th March, 1993
3. **J-Hope** – 18th February, 1994
4. **RM** – 12th September, 1994
5. **Jimin** – 13th October, 1995
6. **V** – 30th December, 1995
7. **Jungkook** – 1st September, 1997

2021

2ND SEPTEMBER

The day Guinness World Records announced BTS had shattered 13 world records in a single year to earn a spot in the 2022 Hall of Fame. "The boys are in the book!" they said. Among the group's triumphs were **'Butter'** becoming the most-streamed track on Spotify in its first 24 hours (11 million plays!) and the boys being crowned the most-followed music group on Instagram.

BACK TO SKOOL

All superheroes have that moment when they magically transform from ordinary people into caped crusaders. For BTS, their big moment was joining Big Hit, an entertainment agency that turned the teenagers from trainees to rookies ... to idols!

BTS =
방탄소년단

IT STARTED WITH A BANG

BTS began with just one rapper – RM. In 2010, Big Hit (now known as HYBE) founder Bang Si-hyuk discovered him after hearing his sharp rhymes in Seoul's underground rap scene. Only 16 at the time, RM impressed Bang so much he became 'the foundation' of BTS. From that moment, Bang envisioned a new type of K-Pop act: "I didn't want them to be false idols," he said. "I wanted to create a BTS that could become a close friend to their fans." And with RM, he had taken the right first step.

The Boys' first TV performance – so cute!

30 BECOMES SEVEN

Before Bang Si-hyuk and RM settled on the final seven, more than 30 trainees rotated through the early BTS lineup – including rapper Iron and producer Supreme Boi. It was a long, uncertain process to find the perfect mix of talent, chemistry and heart. "I promised the members from the very beginning that BTS's music must come from their own stories," Bang Si-hyuk said – and that belief ensured RM, Jin, Suga, J-Hope, Jimin, V and Jungkook would find each other.

LIFE IN THE DORM

Training to become a rookie idol was no easy ride. The seven boys squeezed into a tiny one-room dorm, shared one bathroom and often slept on the floor. Their days ran 16 hours long – dancing, singing, studying English – sometimes surviving on just two hours of sleep. For three years! Each month also brought nerve-racking evaluations where any member could suddenly be cut and a new trainee bought in.

"My goal was always clear: To stand on stage, to become the best. But first, I needed to survive. The trainee period was a constant cycle of having to survive. When one person entered, one person would have to leave. I had to withstand that."

J-Hope, on never giving up on his dream.

School's out! But they won't be rookies for long.

BANGTAN BOMBS

Unlike most idol groups before them, BTS built a large fanbase online before they debuted. They uploaded behind-the-scenes dance practices, freestyle raps and clips to YouTube under *BangtanTV*. These 'Bangtan Bombs' were raw and funny and fans lapped up the authenticity. "When we film the bombs, we're just ourselves and that's what goes up. But it seemed that fans really liked watching our daily life," said Jin.

The boys jump into the mainstream

BEYOND THE SCENE

By late 2012, the name Bangtan Sonyeondan – or Bulletproof Boy Scouts – was made official, symbolising youth's resistance to prejudice and pressure. Before that, names like Big Kidz (short for Big Hit's Kids) and Young Nation were in the mix. In 2017, they rebranded their English name to BTS – Beyond the Scene.

THE FIRST LOGOS

On 27th May, 2013, just weeks before debut, BTS revealed their first official logo: a bulletproof vest, a symbol of protection (from society's 'bullets' of criticism and pressure). On 4th July, 2017, BTS unveiled a sleek new logo: two mirrored trapezoids forming open doors, representing endless possibilities. ARMY received a matching logo too: doors facing BTS, a symbol of protection, unity and the unbreakable connection between the two.

BANG'S GAMBLE

BTS was a huge risk for Big Hit (now HYBE) founder, Bang Si-hyuk. He had written hits for K-Pop act Rain, but by 2010 he wanted his own group. Many ridiculed his vision of a socially conscious hip hop-inspired boy band. Yet Bang trusted RM's talent and assembled seven young hopefuls. "People around me didn't believe in me," Bang said. "They didn't believe I could take this boy group to the top." He proved everyone wrong!

The man with the plan – Bang Si-hyuk!

ALBUM SPOTLIGHT

2 COOL 4 SKOOL

Released on 12th June 2013, BTS's debut paid homage to 1990s hip hop and rap. Through sharp flows and heartfelt, personal lyrics, the boys addressed topics that deeply resonated with South Korea's teenagers.

BOOM BAP!

Big Hit founder Bang Si-hyuk once told RM his destiny was to create a "hip hop idol band" – and *2 Cool 4 Skool* was the sound of that destiny taking shape. The album wore its influences on its sleeves, taking inspiration from many of K-Pop's earliest hip hop pioneers, including Drunken Tiger, Epik High, Dynamic Duo, as well American rappers who made boom bap, rap and trap famous, such as Nas, Jay-Z, Eminem and Lil Wayne.

THE SCHOOL TRILOGY

2 Cool 4 Skool was the first part of BTS's School Trilogy, followed by *O!RUL8,2?* (2013) and *Skool Luv Affair* (2014). The trilogy's lyrical concept was to shine a light on youth struggles and rebellion against the formal, uptight demands of South Korean society.

A THOUGHT FROM SUGA ...

"We started to tell ... the stories that other people could not or would not tell. We said what other people were feeling – like pain, anxieties and worries. That was our goal, to create this empathy that people can relate to." Suga has been open about his depression and wants his fans to know they're not alone.

ROOKIE KINGS

Following the release of *2 Cool 4 Skool*, BTS jumped from the stage to the screen with their own SBS MTV variety show, *Rookie King: Channel Bangtan*. It gave fans a hilarious peek into their rookie personalities. Soon after, they launched *American Hustle Life*, a reality series filmed in Los Angeles where the members learned about US hip hop culture from rap legends such as Coolio and Warren G.

FIRST IMPRESSIONS: THE BAND

During *The Tonight Show Starring Jimmy Fallon* interview in 2020, BTS shared the hilarious story of their first impressions. When Jimmy asked what they thought of each other at first, RM laughed and replied, "When Jungkook first saw me, I was only wearing underwear!" Jimmy, shocked, asked for clarification and RM quickly added, "I mean, in my house!" The story – and Jungkook's blush – had everyone in stitches.

2 COOL 4 SKOOL

1. Intro: 2 Cool 4 Skool (feat. DJ Friz)
2. We Are Bulletproof Pt.2
3. Skit: Circle Room Talk
4. No More Dream
5. Interlude
6. Like (좋아요)
7. Outro: Circle Room Cypher
8. Hidden Track: Skit: On The Start Line
9. Hidden Track: 길 (Road/Path)

THE FIRST FAN: QUEEN OF ARMY

The first ever BTS fan, Mishika Huya, holds the title of 'Queen of ARMY'. Half-Japanese, half-Korean, Mishika was the first leader of ARMY and the first real stan of the band, supporting them even before their official debut. She later became president of the earliest ARMY fan clubs.

TOO COOL FOR SCHOOL

'No More Dream' was BTS's debut single. Written by rappers RM, Suga and J-Hope, the track channels their frustration with South Korea's high-pressure education system and calls out the societal expectation that young people chase 'safe' jobs or admission into elite universities, and fail to dream of anything more. The song was the group's first anthem for dreamers.

No more dreaming for RM

"I don't think our label exactly knew what to do with us!"

RM, on the very early days with J-Hope and RM.

MEMBER SPOTLIGHT JIN

Ladies and Gentleman, meet BTS's eldest vocalist, Kim Seok-jin. Of course, you might know him by another name: Worldwide Handsome!

LUCKY DAY

Jin's road to BTS was a true twist of fate! One lucky day in 2011, while stepping off a bus on his way to Konkuk University, a Big Hit staff member spotted him and thought, "That face belongs on stage!" Scouted purely for his appearance at first, Jin had no singing or dance experience but gave the audition a shot anyway. Two days after Jin (aged 18) joined, Jungkook followed – making the oldest and youngest trainees six years apart upon their debut.

STREET-CAST TWICE

Before K-Pop stardom, Jin dreamed of being a K-Drama star. In his second year of high school, he was inspired to study film and act after watching Kim Nam-gil in *Queen Seondeok* (2009). While at middle school, Jin was actually scouted first by SM Entertainment – one of Big Hit's biggest rivals – but he turned it down to focus on his film studies.

HEIGHT: 179cm / 5'10"

****

FAVE FOOD: Lobster, sashimi

****

FAVE TV: *Dragon Ball* and *Parasyte*

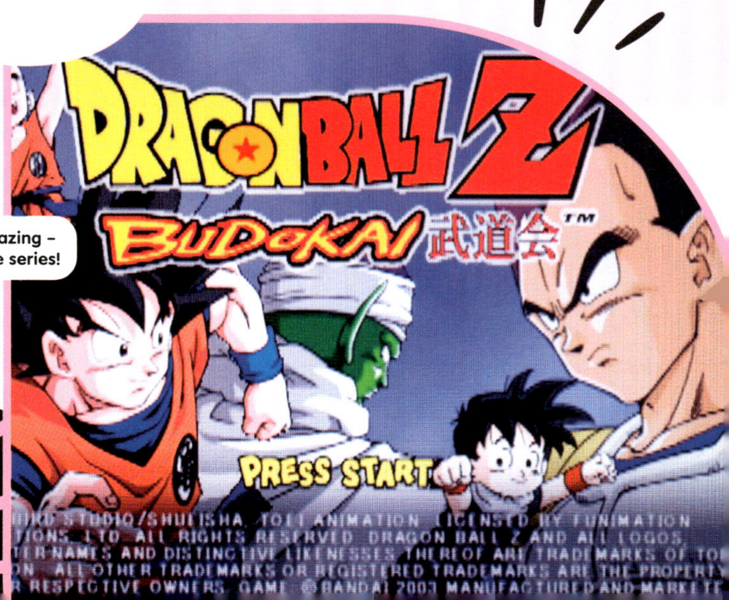

Dragonball is amazing – a must-see anime series!

Jin lights up Paris for the Olympics, 2024.

THE MAGNIFICENT SEVEN!

With seven No. 1 songs on Billboard's World Digital Song Sales chart, Jin holds the Guinness World record for the most by any solo artist. Can you name the seven?

Answers:
1. 'Yours', 2. 'Super Tuna', 3. 'The Astronaut',
4. 'I'll Be There', 5. 'Heart on the Window',
6. 'Falling', 7. 'Close to You'.

"I want to emphasize, for the record, that during my audition everybody went berserk about how good-looking I was!"

JIN, keeping things humble!

DAD JOKE JOKER

Jin is the undisputed king of dad jokes, or *ajae gaegŭ* (아재개그). These are his best. (Sorry, make that his worst!)

1. What do you give a cannibal when he's late for supper? *A cold shoulder!*
2. What do you call a cat that goes to space? *Rockat!*
3. What colour is a burger? *Burgundy!*

Big Jin on the side of a massive building!

LOST IN SPACE

In October 2022, Jin made his long-awaited solo debut with **'The Astronaut'**. The track was no ordinary song. It was co-written with Chris Martin, from the beloved British rock band Coldplay, who had previously teamed up with Jin and the boys on **'My Universe'** in 2021. It holds a record in Korea for selling more than 700,000 copies on its first day. Crazy!

INSTANT NOODLE MUKBANG!

On his days off, Jin is almost certainly cooking and eating! Since 2015, his 'Eat Jin' livestreams have become ARMY favourites. Labelled *mukbang*, a Korean trend where hosts eat on camera while chatting with viewers. The series became so beloved that he was named global ambassador for *Ottogi Jin Instant Noodles* – and he's even joked about modelling on the packaging someday!

WORLDWIDE HANDSOME

Jin famously dubbed himself "Worldwide Handsome" – and the nickname stuck! (Because it's true!) He first used the name jokingly during a 2017 press event and later repeated it so confidently that it became part of his identity with ARMY.

Jin using his noodle as always!

ALBUM SPOTLIGHT

DARK & WILD

The sound of seven rookies kicking down K-Pop's doors, demanding to be heard, *Dark & Wild* is the perfect intro to the former hip hop crew – BTS! Enter ... if you dare!

THE BIG BANG

Released on 19th August, 2014, *Dark & Wild* was BTS's first full-length Korean studio album. At the time, the group was still fighting for recognition (and respect!), against K-Pop giants such as EXO, Girls' Generation and BigBang from far larger agencies. With limited money but limitless ambition, BTS set out to make noise – and did they ever! *Dark & Wild* smashed K-Pop norms with raw hip hop, trap, boom bap and even grunge – genres rarely heard in idol music then.

A WALK ON THE WILD SIDE

Dark & Wild is an album of two halves: anger and passion. The first seven tracks burn with frustration and jealousy. The latter half explores the wild, unrestrained side of desire. "We created the track list from start to finish with the hope that fans would listen to it all the way through," RM explained. "The interlude is the midpoint – before it's 'dark,' after it's 'wild.'" Designed to flow like a cinematic story, the album is meant to be listened to in order.

DANGER, BEWARE!

"Lead singles always dictate the theme of the rest of the album," RM said of **'Danger'** – and this one set the tone with a bang! The music video is pure wild fun: the boys' stomp through a graffiti-splashed subway tunnel, smashing walls and dancing next to flaming shopping carts. The MV was filmed partly in an abandoned school building in Seoul, used in several Korean horror films, and rumoured to have been haunted to boot.

BTS paint the town red - in their inimitable style!

A THOUGHT FROM RM ...

"I've had to accept that everyone cannot love me. Because when there's love there's hate, when there's light there's dark. But it was really hard to accept as an artist that there's a lot of people that hate me but ... there are many more people who love me." RM is philosophical about the darker side of fame.

JAPANESE ALBUMS

From *Dark & Wild* onward, BTS began releasing Japanese-language albums in tandem with their Korean albums, a move to reach Japan's massive music market. Each of these albums blended re-recorded songs with brand-new Japanese originals. There is: *Wake Up* (2014), *Youth* (2016), *Face Yourself* (2018), *Map of the Soul: 7 – The Journey* (2020), each one as essential as the last.

DARK & WILD

1. Intro: What Am I To You
2. Danger
3. War of Hormone
4. Hip Hop Phile
5. Let Me Know
6. Rain
7. BTS Cypher Pt.3: Killer (ft. Supreme Boi)
8. Interlude: What Are You Doing Now
9. Could You Turn Off Your Cell Phone
10. Embarrassed
11. 24/7=Heaven
12. Look Here
13. So 4 More
14. Outro: Do You Think It Makes Sense?

Don't just stand there – say something, boys!

CYPHER SWAGGER!

From **'BTS Cypher Pt.1'** on *O!RUL8,2?* (2013) to **'BTS Cypher Pt.4'** on *Wings* (2016), BTS's rap line – RM, Suga and J-Hope – showcased their rapid-fire rap skills and sharp wordplay on tracks known as cyphers. Each cypher delivers an opportunity for the rappers to spit hard-hitting verses aimed at critics and haters that are more than just diss tracks: they're a reminder that BTS's hip hop roots run deep.

"Our music criticizes the bad points of society and pokes fun at it a lot. That side of us was dark. And we also always wore dark clothes."

RM, reminiscing about the band's early style.

BRAVE THE STAGE

Thrilling live performers, the boys have played more than 300 concerts since 2013. These are the seven shows that mattered the most ...

FIRST US STADIUM SHOW

6th October, 2018 – the date BTS made history when they became the first K-Pop act to headline a US stadium, New York's Citi Field. The band performed to 40,000 fans and tickets sold out in a matter of seconds!

The boys were over the moon to perform in the US

AY, OH, WEMBLEY!

On 1st–2nd June, 2019, BTS became the first Korean act to headline London's iconic Wembley Stadium, performing to more than 80,000 fans each night! The concerts were also livestreamed to more than 140,000 viewers worldwide, making it one of the most-watched music events ever. In classic Jin mode, his now-legendary 'Ay-Oh' chant paid tribute to Freddie Mercury's Live Aid moment from 1985, a defining (and deafening!) milestone in pop history.

Can you spot any other idols in this picture?

YET TO COME

In October 2022, South Korea's Busan Asiad Main Stadium hosted BTS's final full-group concert before their military service – a night bursting with fireworks, illuminated drones and 100,000 emotional fans. Watched by **nearly 50 million viewers** worldwide via WeVerse, it also became one of the largest online gatherings in music history. Onstage, Jimin fought back tears as he told his fans: "I believe what we've done so far is just a taste. We should keep going – 30, 40, 70 years!"

"When we began touring and performing in front of live audiences all over the world, we felt that we had evolved one step further in our journey as artists."

Suga knows the importance of performing live.

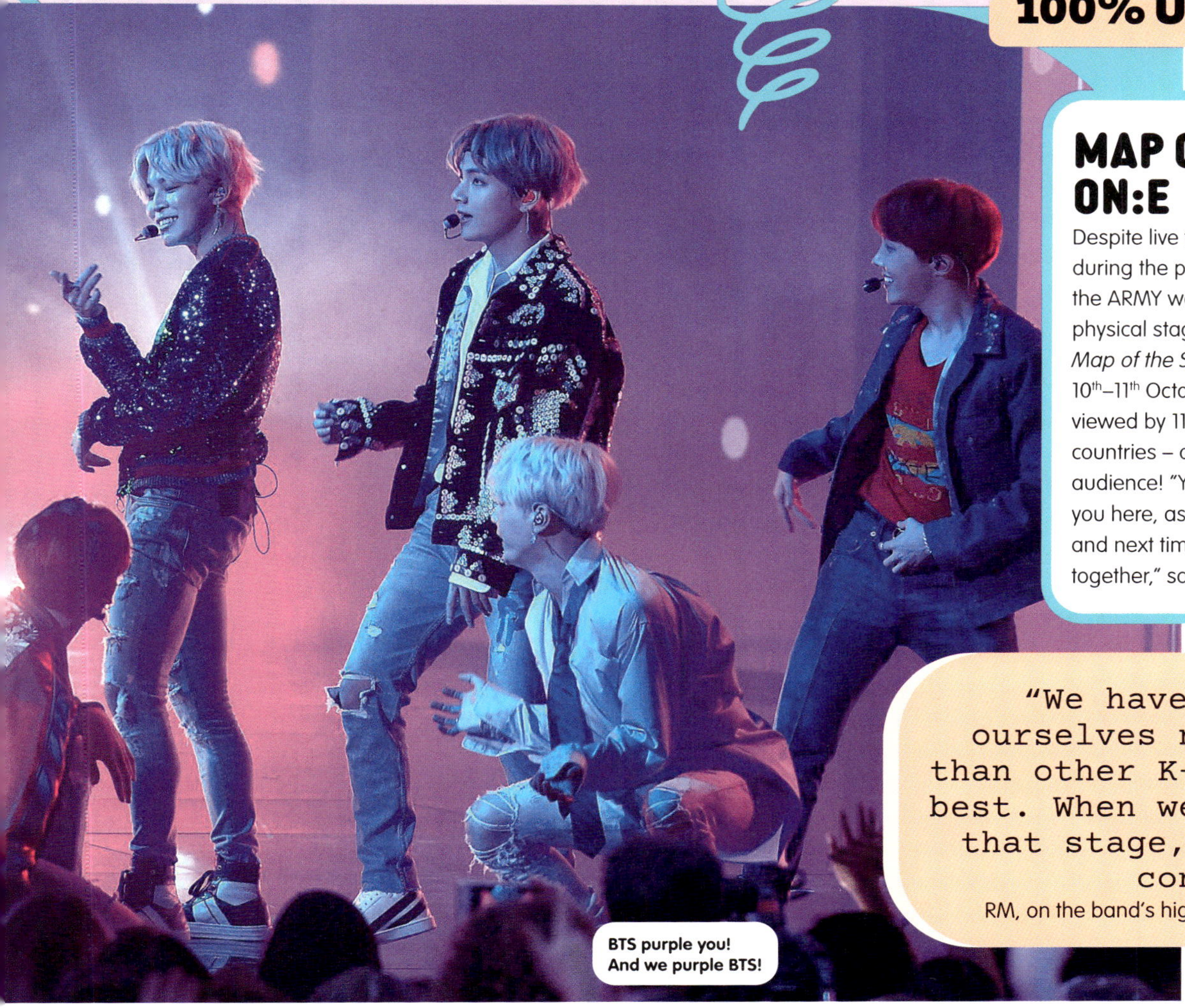

BTS purple you! And we purple BTS!

MAP OF THE SOUL ON:E

Despite live touring being halted during the pandemic, BTS still united the ARMY worldwide without a physical stage. They put on the *Map of the Soul ON:E* concert on 10th–11th October, 2020, a livestream viewed by 114 million fans across 191 countries – a record-breaking digital audience! "You're not here but I feel you here, as if I can hear your chants and next time let's really be here together," said an emotional V.

"We have to consider ourselves not just better than other K-Pop acts but the best. When we're out there on that stage, we're there to conquer."

RM, on the band's high expectations for themselves.

BTS-MANIA!

When BTS appeared on *The Late Show* with Stephen Colbert on 15th May, 2019, pop history came full circle. On the very same stage where The Beatles performed their legendary 1964 debut to more than 60 million viewers on the Ed Sullivan Show, BTS lit it up with **'Boy With Luv'**. Dressed in matching black suits and skinny ties – the same as The Beatles – they paid playful homage to the Fab Four.

DIONYSUS LIVES

At South Korea's Melon Music Awards (MMA), on 30th November, 2019, BTS delivered their most ambitious performance – a 37-minute mini-show spectacular that fused Greek mythology with super-sharp choreography over six songs, including **'Intro: Persona'**, **'Boy With Luv'**, **'Mikrokosmos'** and **'Dionysus'**. ARMY still hail it as one of K-Pop's most iconic performances.

AMERICAN MUSIC AWARDS

On 19th November, 2017, the boys performed **'DNA'** at the 2017 AMAs, becoming the first K-Pop group to perform at the show. More than 10 million people watched them. The show marked BTS's US award-show debut and launched them into American mainstream consciousness. "The AMAs were the biggest gift we could have gotten from our fans," said Suga on the night.

Camera ready! The BTS boys strike a pose!

BEHIND THE STYLE

From baggy hip hop streetwear to sharp monochrome suits, the Bangtan Boys have worn it all – and made it all look good! These are their seven style eras ... which is your favourite?

In their Luxe era: J-Hope is dubbed the 'fashion king' by the band.

2013 - 2014

HIP HOP ROOKIE ERA

Debut-era BTS – classic! For their first year, the group dripped with hip hop swagger dressed in oversized basketball jerseys, all-black streetwear, snapback caps, bandanas, chunky gold chains and heavy eyeliner, an instantly recognisable identity distinct from other K-Pop idol groups.

Dancing with style in the early days.

2014

SCHOOL UNIFORM ERA

With *Skool Luv Affair* and *2 Cool 4 Skool,* BTS embraced stylised school uniforms – blazers, ties, shirts and trainers. The look perfectly reflected their early albums' 'schoolboy crush' concept. Which member wore it best, though?

Back to the classroom! They look so young!

2015 - 2016

The era when they became global stars.

YOUTH ERA

With the *Most Beautiful Moment in Life* era, BTS shifted gears. Think pastel cardigans, soft knitwear, floral shirts and bomber jackets. Pure poetry in motion.

"They go well together: powerful music, colourful clothes."

Suga knows music and style go hand in hand.

2016

DARK & EDGY ERA

The *Wings* era turned BTS dark, decadent and devilish! Dressed in burgundy, emerald and black satin shirts, velvet blazers, chokers and leather pants, the style beautifully mirrored the album's themes of temptation. This was BTS's most daring style shift yet.

Looking smokin' hot in their new outfits!

2017 - 2018

SHARP SUIT ERA

With the *Love Yourself* trilogy, BTS's transformation to international style icons was complete. Sleek, sharp-fitting monochrome suits, metallic blazers and embroidered jackets became the norm. Their entrance at the 2018 Billboard Music Awards and other American TV debuts spotlighted their desire for pin-sharp tailoring.

Boys to Men: sharp suits and shiny boots.

2019 - 2020

SUNSHINE AND SPARKLE ERA

With **'Dynamite'** came a blast of candy-coloured retro joy! BTS swapped their darker look for neon suits, disco shirts and funky flared pants straight out of the '70s. It was pure feel-good energy!

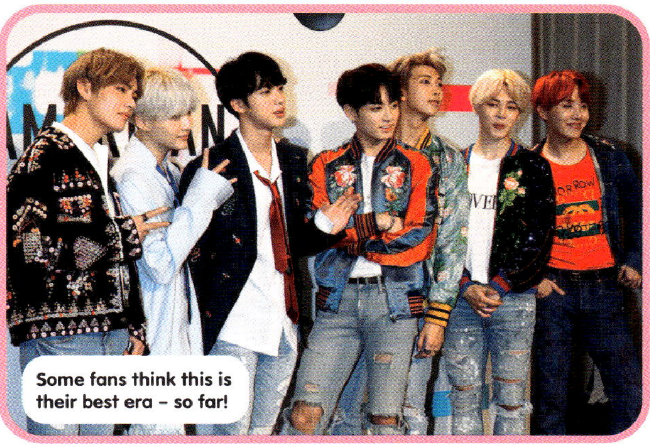

Some fans think this is their best era – so far!

2019 - 2020

MODERN LUXE ERA

Appointed Louis Vuitton ambassadors in 2021, BTS dripped in sleek leather, tailored outerwear and slim luxury fits from the world's finest fashion houses such as LV, Dior and Gucci. Fancy!

The band even looked great in their military service uniforms!

MEMBER SPOTLIGHT → SUGA

The band's resident chief of big beats, Min Yoongi, or Suga, is also the group's most thoughtful spokesperson for positive change.

SPEAK YOUR TRUTH

Suga's love affair with hip hop began in 2005, when he was 12 years old and first heard Stony Skunk's **'Ragga Muffin'**. By 13, Suga was crafting his own beats! From there, Suga was influenced by Kanye West, Lil Wayne and Eminem, rappers with a gift for speaking the blunt truth. "To me, hip hop is a culture of being honest," Suga has said. "It's not about bragging about being rich or owning a gold chain, but a genre where we can speak honestly about our generation and what they think."

HEIGHT: 174cm / 5'9"

****

FAVE FOOD: Galbi (Korean beef short ribs)

****

FAVE TV: *Naruto* and *Slam Dunk*

RAP WRITER

Suga has been writing down raps in his notebooks since elementary school, despite hip hop being relatively unknown, or unpopular, in Korea at the time. "There probably wasn't anyone else on the streets who rapped, except for me. Since there wasn't anyone who rapped, I thought I was the best!" he has said. Today, the Korea Music Copyright Association credits Suga with more than 160 registered songs, making him one of K-Pop's most prolific songwriters.

Suga's very own private idol – Eminem!

We think Suga is oh so sweet!

BIG HIT WITH BIG HIT

Suga's journey to BTS began with Big Hit's 'Hit It' audition in his hometown of Daegu. He was accepted the very next day! "I wanted to debut and become a singer and do my music as a trainee. There was never a moment when I didn't have that dream," he later said. Originally training as a producer alongside Supreme Boi, Suga's sharp rap skills quickly stood out.

ARISE, SIR AGUST D!

In 2016, Suga unveiled his first solo mixtape, *Agust D*, a collection of rage-fuelled rapid-fire raps! The name itself is a clever mirror: *Agust D* comes from 'DT' (Daegu Town) and 'Suga' reversed, meant to represent his underground origins. "*Agust D* might be a more accurate depiction of who I really am … it allows me to freely express my thoughts," Suga has said of his alter ego.

SHINING LIKE A STAR

Before joining Big Hit as a trainee, Suga was already making waves in Daegu's underground hip hop scene. Performing under the name Gloss, he was part of the crew D-Town, short for 'Daegu Town'. The name Gloss suited him perfectly: The word echoed the English meaning of his Korean surname, *Yoongi*, which translates to 'shine'.

He's probably thinking of his bed – his favourite place.

SUGAR, SUGAR

Suga's stage name doesn't come from the fact that he's sweet like sugar – though, obviously, he is! It comes from the Korean syllables for shooting guard, the position he played in basketball at school. "Shooting guard = Su-Ga," he revealed on Jimmy Fallon's *Tonight Show* in 2024.

SUGARY TREATS

Suga has become one of Korea's most successful solo performers ever! His debut studio album *D-Day* (2023) debuted at No. 2 on the Billboard 200, tying Jimin as the highest-charting South Korean soloist. The album's world tour, *D-Day: The Tour*, sold out arenas across Asia, the US and beyond, making Suga the first BTS member to headline a solo world tour!

> "If we don't talk about these issues, who will? Who knows best and can talk about the difficulty our generation faces? It's us."

Suga, on the band's responsibility to speak for their generation.

ALBUM SPOTLIGHT

THE MOST BEAUTIFUL MOMENT IN LIFE, PT. 1

Released on 29th April, 2015, this album records the moment the Bangtan Boys transformed from rookie caterpillars to beautiful game-changing butterflies!

HWA YANG YEON HWA

HWA YANG YEON HWA, or 花樣年華, in Korean, translates to 'The Most Beautiful Moment in Life', the 'flower-like' blossoming of a person's youth. For this album, the boys moved away from the fast-paced angst of hip hop into the more upbeat world of pop. The result is BTS's first (of many!) artistic leaps and showcased a much more polished sound.

"Youth is the most beautiful moment in life. We're delivering stories of people our age through music."

RM explains their appeal.

THE BTS UNIVERSE

Starting with *The Most Beautiful Moment in Life, Pt.1* album, the group began the BTS Universe (BU), or Bangtan Universe, a fictional story that links together all of BTS's albums, music videos and short films into one emotional saga. The narrative follows seven characters navigating love, loss and fate while trying to save one another. In addition to the music and MVs there was also the *Save Me* webtoon, short stories, books and *The Notes*, a series of diary entries from each member of the band.

The most beautiful band in the world!

THE MOST BEAUTIFUL MOMENT IN LIFE, PT. 1

1. Intro: The Most Beautiful Moment in Life
2. I Need U
3. Hold Me Tight
4. Skit: Expectation!
5. DOPE
6. Boyz with Fun
7. Converse High
8. Moving On
9. Outro: Love Is Not Over

Which member would you like to meet first?

A THOUGHT FROM SUGA ...

"I would like more talented Korean artists to be better known around the world, because there are a lot of talented Korean artists and it's really amazing to have this small country and so many talented people coming out of it." Suga is a passionate advocate for the Korean music scene. **Part One** certainly helped bring K-Pop into the mainstream. Job done, Suga!

HIGH HOPES

The most fun song in the BTS canon isn't **'Boyz With Fun'** (though that's a close second!) – it's **'Converse High'**! In this cheeky track, RM gives off massive crush energy about a girl who looks perfect in just her Converse high tops, jeans and a white tee! Thankfully, Jungkook never followed up with an ode to his once beloved Timberlands – some footwear fantasies are best left unwritten!

JIN IS ALWAYS RIGHT!

"*The Most Beautiful Moment in Life Pt.1* was the album that first allowed us to win awards at music shows in Korea and attract more fans. Nobody expected it to be a massive hit, but it became a key stepping stone for us moving onward. We're not completely sure why it was this specific album that played that role," Jimin has said of its importance. Jin knew the album was going to be a success because J-Hope said it *wouldn't* – and every time he says that, Jin knows the opposite happens!

FOREVER YOUNG

The HYYH era – as it is known – covered a trilogy of albums, starting with *The Most Beautiful Moment in Life, Pt. 1* and *Pt. 2* in 2015 and then the compilation album *Young Forever* in 2016, which contained three new tracks, including **'Save Me'** and **'Fire'**. In just over a year, the band released 22 new songs, making them also the most prolific K-Pop band to beat.

BEHOLD THE SCREAMS!

ARMY is a global cultural movement of fans so loyal to BTS they deserve their own purple hearts!

ARMY IS AN ACRONYM

ARMY is more than just millions of loyal fans, they are BTS's unstoppable superhero soldier squad! The name ARMY stands for 'Adorable Representative M.C. for Youth'. If you're truly in the ARMY, you'll be able to answer this: there is only one member of BTS that has the word 'ARMY' tattooed on his knuckles? Who is it? Jungkook, of course!

BTS love ARMY – and that means YOU!

ARMY – ASSEMBLE! Wherever the boys are, ARMY will be.

MATCH A MILLION

ARMY's greatest moment (so far!) came in June 2020 when millions of fans mobilised the #MatchAMillion challenge after BTS donated $1 million to the Black Lives Matter movement. The goal? Raise the same amount in 24 hours. The result? $1,026,531.80 – mission accomplished! The campaign demonstrated, for the first time, the power of a pop group's fandom and its ability to create positive social change.

BANGTAN TV

Before stadium shows, BTS got up close with ARMY through a screen. BangtanTV, their official YouTube channel, launched on 17th December, 2012. Their first upload was a rap video by RM called **'Vote'**, encouraging young people in South Korea to vote. Pretty soon it became the group's digital diary, from dance practice chaos to travel vlogs to goofy challenges. BangtanTV now has more than 80 million subscribers and 25 billion views.

SQUAD GOALS

Just how big is ARMY? It's MASSIVE. Around 40 per cent of the global K-Pop audience (roughly 150 million people!) are believed to be just BTS fans. That means ARMY could number around 60 million worldwide, bigger than the population of Spain! If ARMY were a real army, it would be the largest army on Earth.

Dutch ARMY shows up for BTS!

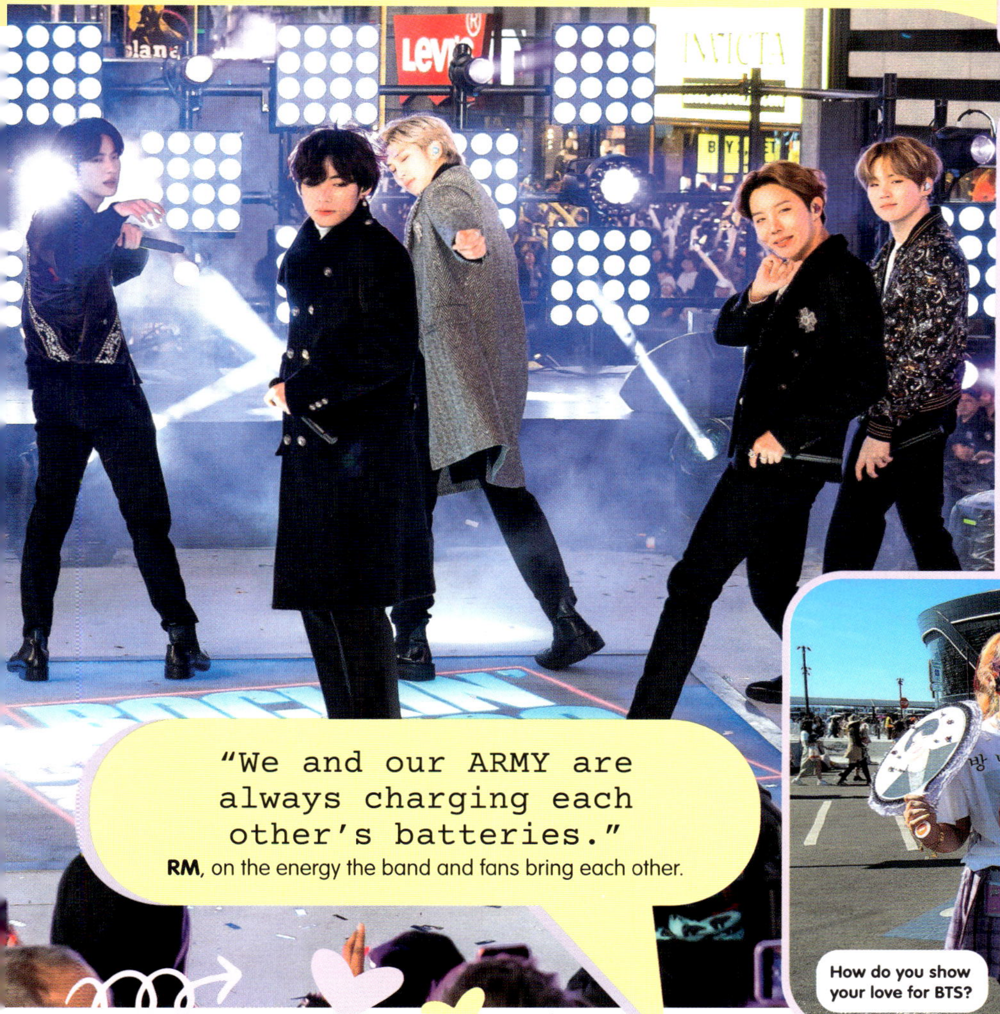

BTS FESTA

Every June, BTS FESTA turns K-Pop's 'Seven-Year Curse' on its head. (Many idol groups disappear after seven years – the length of a standard idol contract). But BTS keeps growing! FESTA, every June, is their band's month-long love letter to ARMY, with loads of new photos, content and heartfelt messages to their fans. In 2025, the celebration was the biggest it's ever been with a convention in Goyang, South Korea, complete with interactive zones and a dazzling light show. See you there next year!

"We and our ARMY are always charging each other's batteries."

RM, on the energy the band and fans bring each other.

How do you show your love for BTS?

OT7 BTS

This means loving **all seven** members – equally, endlessly and as one. Standing for 'One True 7', it's a fan's pledge of unity, celebrating BTS as a complete team no matter who's on stage, or having success as a solo artist. 'OT7' reminds ARMY that BTS's magic comes from all seven hearts beating together: seven voices, one story, forever Bangtan!

SONGS FOR THE ARMY

'2! 3!' from *Wings* was BTS's first official love letter to ARMY. Ever since, BTS have written songs with lyrics directed directly at their ARMY, including **'Magic Shop'** (2018), **'Mikrokosmos'** (2019) and **'We Are Bulletproof: The Eternal'** (2020). Which one is your favourite?

AWARD-WINNING ARMY

BTS's fandom is so powerful, it needs its own trophy shelf! At the iHeartRadio Music Awards, ARMY has snagged 'Best Fan Army' seven years in a row (2018–2024) – an unbeatable streak! At the MTV Europe Music Awards, they've claimed five 'Biggest Fans' wins since 2015. Even Radio Disney crowned ARMY the 'Fiercest Fans' in 2018. The ARMY-mania in 2026 is going to be even more bonkers, so get ready for action!

What does YOUR sign say? Admit it: you've made one.

BTS's stylist had one job: to buy one grey suit x 7.

ALBUM SPOTLIGHT

WINGS

The album that catapulted BTS into world domination in October 2016, *Wings* could not be more aptly named: it sent the boys flying high!

BROKEN WINGS

WINGS took flight with a little literary magic – straight from Hermann Hesse's 1919 classic *Demian*. The novel's mix of sin, self-discovery and salvation runs right through this era. In *Demian*, young Emil Sinclair meets the mysterious Max Demian, who opens his eyes to the wild duality of human nature – light and dark, good and evil – and angels with broken wings. Sound familiar?

SEE THE BAND SOAR

When *Wings* landed, BTS revealed it was about "falling into temptation and losing innocence" – and fans couldn't resist either! The album flew straight to No. 1 in Korea, becoming their first million-seller. Suddenly, the boys were as big as their own idols – 2NE1, EXO and even Psy. "BTS are giving Korea many proud moments," Psy said of BTS. "And, honestly, I'm proud too!"

All together now: "Op, Op, Op, Oppa is Gangnam Style!"

SEVEN STORIES AS ONE

With *Wings*, for the first time, every BTS member got their own solo on a full album. Suga's cinematic **'First Love'**; Jimin's **'Lie'** dripped with drama; V's **'Stigma'** oozed soul-infused jazz; RM's **'Reflection'** wrestled his self-doubt; J-Hope's **'Mama'** glowed with gratitude for his mum; and Jin's **'Awake'** ached with vulnerability. Every album since has copied the format.

BLOOD. SWEAT. TEARS.

The MV for **'Blood Sweat & Tears'** smashed records with more than six million views in just 24 hours – the fastest K-Pop video to hit that milestone! "The song relays an optimistic determination to use our wings to go far, even if we are met with temptations in life," revealed Suga.

MOOMBAHTON!

If you had to define what *Wings* sounds like, you might call it moombahton! It's when house and reggaeton meet. It's not a Korean word, or something Jin might eat. Moombahton was born in the US in 2009 and BTS sprinkled it across *Wings* to make their music sound more global.

FLY WITH ME

'Begin', Jungkook's solo track, is a beautiful love letter to his BTS brothers. ARMY consider it a musical hug from the golden *maknae* to the *hyungs* (his older brothers in the band) who helped him grow. "When I was fifteen years old, I had nothing. The world was too big and I was small," he sings. Kookie sings his thanks for helping him "discover my emotions". Sweet.

PLAY IT AGAIN ...

1. Intro: Boy Meets Evil
2. Blood Sweat & Tears
3. Begin
4. Lie
5. Stigma
6. First Love
7. Reflection
8. MAMA
9. Awake
10. Lost
11. BTS Cypher 4
12. Am I Wrong
13. 21st Century Girl
14. Two! Three! (Hoping for Better Days)
15. Interlude: Wings

A THOUGHT FROM RM ...

"For the *Wings* album, we are telling side stories from seven different perspectives. We wanted to show different looks with sweet hair colour changes to look younger, brighter and warmer too." RM shows us that when telling their stories, the styling of the band is often just as important as the music.

PANSORI PEOPLE

Pansori is a traditional Korean genre of musical storytelling performed by a single vocalist and a drummer. It combines singing, narration and dramatic gestures to tell an epic story, with performances sometimes lasting for hours. The name 'pansori' is composed of the Korean words pan (meaning 'open space') and sori (meaning 'song'). *Wings* has it in spades with all the solo songs.

MEMBER SPOTLIGHT J-HOPE

Jung Hoseok is a pure ray of sunshine, he is adored by everyone for his bright, positive personality that keeps the group's spirits soaring. Say hello to 'mother' – J-Hope!

JUNG IN A BOX

J-Hope's real name, Jung, is a common Korean name that actually means affection and warmth, qualities J-Hope is famed for. The name J-Hope also carries a deeper symbolism, inspired by the Greek myth of Pandora's Box. "You know how in Pandora's Box after everything else left, the only thing remaining was hope, right? I put 'hope' in my name to be a hopeful existence in the group," J-Hope has said.

HEIGHT: 177cm / 5'10"

****

FAVE FOOD: Kimchi fried rice, bibimbap

****

FAVE TV: *Infinite Challenge*

POP AND LOCK

Before his debut, J-Hope was a rising star in Gwangju's underground dance scene. He joined the dance crew Neuron and studied at Gwangju Music Academy for six years. "I did a lot of popping!" he said. In 2008, he won first place at a national dance contest, a win that led him to idol training with Big Hit. "When I was a little kid, I simply loved expressing myself with my body. Everyone liked me when I went up on the stage at a talent search in elementary school and that's when I decided to become a music artist."

We think someone (J-Hope) might need a new shirt!

A ray of Hope! J-Hope keeps the sun shining.

HOPE IS GREEN

Ever since his debut, J-Hope has been associated with the colour green, his favourite colour. Each member has their own favourite colour. Jungkook's is red; V's is purple; Jimin's is blue; RM's is black; Suga's is white; Jin's is pink. Which member matches with your favourite colour?

Do you believe in Hope? We do!

ONE-MAN SUNSHINE BAND

During idol training, it was J-Hope who found the process the hardest. At one point, he left the lineup due to feeling overwhelmed and exhausted. In *Burn the Stage*, the group recall this moment. Jungkook cried at the thought of his friend leaving. Thankfully, RM persuaded him to return. "I can't imagine what we would be without him," RM said. "J-Hope always tries to cheer us up and I'm so grateful. I like to call him the new leader of the group."

"It's still unbelievable that our singing and dancing, which we began out of pure enjoyment, has spread such an impact across the world."

J-Hope hasn't forgotten where BTS started.

HOBIPALOOZA

On 31st July, 2022, J-Hope made history as the first Korean artist ever to headline a major US music festival: Chicago's Lollapalooza. His awesome 90-minute solo set drew more than 100,000 fans! Onstage, J-Hope admitted the gig was "my greatest and most unforgettable moment", though also admitted it was "one dread-filled moment after another – an hour-long show with me front and centre!" Luckily, his BFF Jimin was in the crowd cheering him on!

SEVEN SONGS

J-Hope's favourite songs …

1. 'No More Dream'
2. 'Boy In Luv'
3. 'DOPE'
4. 'FIRE'
5. 'Save Me'
6. 'Blood Sweat & Tears'
7. 'Not Today'

FIRST TO GO SOLO

J-Hope was the first BTS member to release a full solo studio album with *Jack in the Box* on 15th July, 2022. It set a high bar for BTS's solo albums, that's for sure!

Checking in on J-Hope. Are you all-white?

BETWEEN THE SCREENS

With more than 70 music videos on YouTube, the Bangtan Boys have turned their musical storytelling into visual masterpieces. Don't believe us? Check these MVs out.

'NO MORE DREAM'

BTS's debut music video is "hella lit" (to quote RM!). It has more than 325 million views. **'No More Dream'** features the band, dressed in basketball gear and large gold chains, crashing a school bus and hip hopping all over a graffiti-covered school! Too cool for school? Oh yeah!

BTS run riot in the classroom in their first MV.

MV = Music Video

Snog Marry Avoid – who would you choose?

'I NEED U'

With more five million likes and 200 million views, **'I NEED U'** was the lead single from *The Most Beautiful Moment in Life, Pt. 1*. The MV was the first to explore the members grappling with pain, loneliness and despair, blending realism with haunting images. A later 19+ rated version was even released and included two minutes of darker, more graphic scenes.

"Mirror, Mirror on the wall, who's the greatest idol of them all?"

Keeping warm the BTS way – just dance it out!

'SAVE ME'

Filmed as a single continuous take, **'Save Me'** uses killer choreography as storytelling with the boys' bodies conveying desperation and hope all at the same time against a backdrop of clouds and low-light. Since the news of the group's reunion in 2026, ARMY have tried their best to get the video to one billion views, as it deserves.

Can you do the iconic DNA whistle?

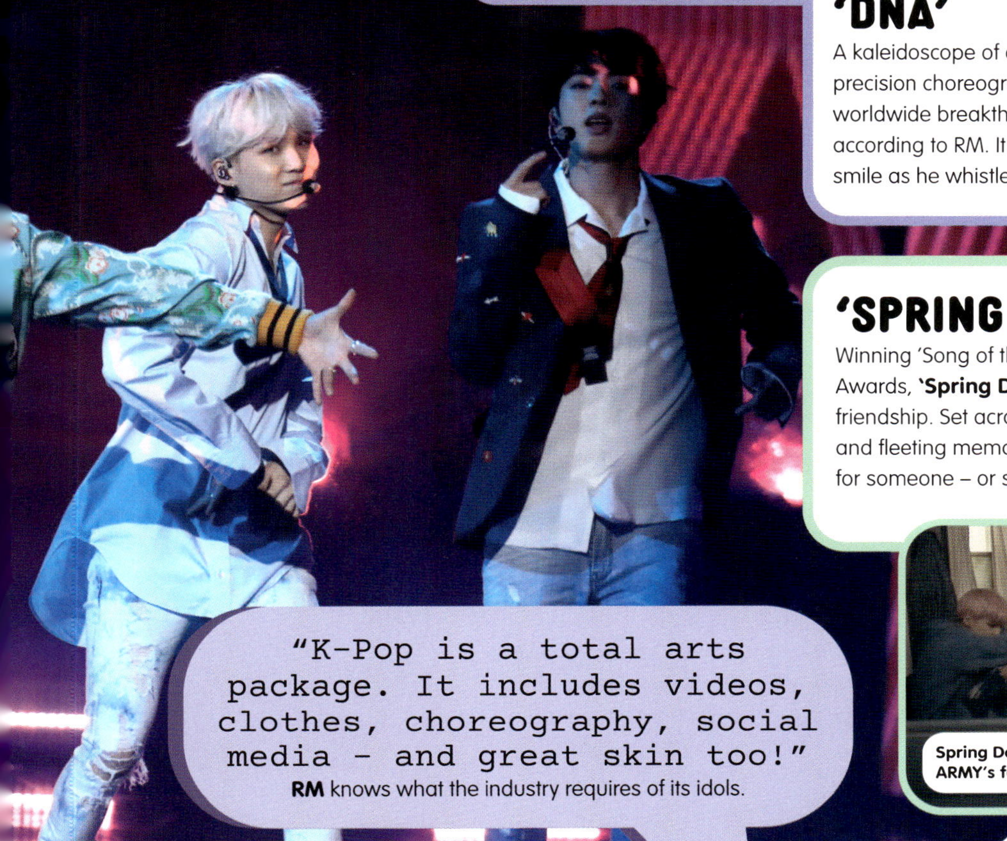

“K-Pop is a total arts package. It includes videos, clothes, choreography, social media – and great skin too!”
RM knows what the industry requires of its idols.

‘DNA’

A kaleidoscope of cosmic and mind-bending visuals and military precision choreography, **‘DNA’** was the MV that marked BTS’s worldwide breakthrough and the group’s second chapter, according to RM. It has more than 1.5 billion views. Jungkook’s smile as he whistles makes ARMY go mad every time!

‘SPRING DAY’

Winning ‘Song of the Year’ award at the 2017 Melon Music Awards, **‘Spring Day’** is a poetic story of loss, longing and friendship. Set across wintry landscapes, empty train stations and fleeting memories, it follows the members as they search for someone – or something – missing.

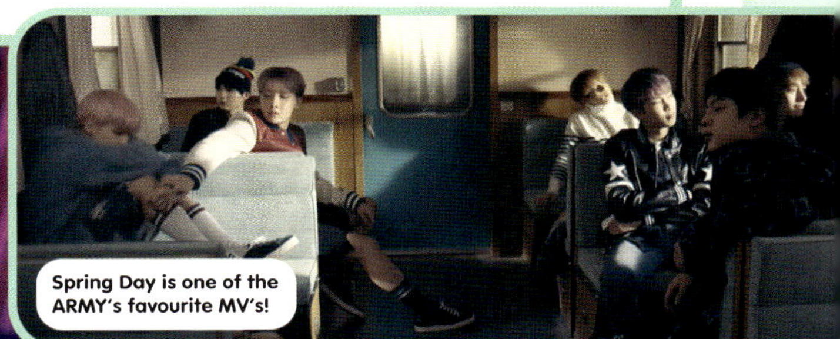

Spring Day is one of the ARMY’s favourite MV’s!

‘PERMISSION TO DANCE’

The wait is over! Set in a hope-filled, post-pandemic world, the MV to **‘Permission to Dance’** bursts with positivity, purple balloons and the boys dressed like cowboys! The best bit? When everyone takes off their masks and dances like crazy! The song may have been written by Ed Sheeran but it’s positive energy is pure BTS.

Hands down the Best. Video. Ever.

Can you do the Black Swan dance?

‘BLACK SWAN’

Inspired by the Oscar-winning movie of the same name, **‘Black Swan’** sees the band dressed in white attire, interacting with their dark shadows. The choreography is acclaimed by ARMY as being the group’s best to date!

BTS’S FAVOURITE MV’S

1. ‘Young Forever’
2. ‘FIRE’
3. ‘Run’
4. ‘Save Me’
5. ‘Spring Day’
6. ‘ON’
7. ‘Dynamite’

BORN TO SINGI

Seven tours and counting – with an eighth kickstarted in spring 2026! – BTS's life on the road has given more than six million ARMY members a load of amazing moments, just like these ...

CATCH A BULLET

The boys' first ever concert tour was called the *Red Bullet*! It began on 17th October, 2014, in South Korea and saw the group perform to just 5,000 fans. When the group extended the tour to America a few months later, the first shows sold out in just two minutes!

MEETING UP WITH ARMY

29th March, 2014 – the day the band held their very first BTS Global Official Fanclub meeting in Seoul. Thousands of ARMY soldiers turned up to watch the group perform songs, play games and share stories. For many fans, that day was the beginning of BTS's legendary bond with their ARMY. Were you there?

CALIFORNIA DREAMING

The band's first ever stadium tour – the *Love Yourself World Tour* – kicked off at a sold-out show at America's iconic Rose Bowl in Pasadena, California. They played to more than 110,000 fans and sold out the show in under ten minutes!

IN-FLIGHT ENTERTAINMENT

Starting and ending at Seoul's 22,000-capacity Gocheok Sky Dome, the boys most ambitious tour, 2017's *The Wings Tour,* performed to more than 500,000 fans! During the shows, each member had their own stages for their solo songs. On the final night, Suga broke down in tears in front of the fans: "I sincerely thought that there was going to be nothing to cry about, but I'm feeling a bit emotional at the end of our tour," he said. "BTS started, full of aspirations of fighting against oppression and prejudice. I'm thankful that many can hear our music." Bless!

Seeing BTS live? Don't forget your *Eungwonbong* (응원봉), your official tour fan light stick!

PERMISSION TO DANCE – AGAIN!

After more than a year of virtual shows, BTS reunited with ARMY through their *Permission to Dance On Stage* concerts. Their four-night run at Los Angeles' SoFi Stadium played to more than 800,000 fans and it is now considered one of their most important shows. In fact, it was so good, they made a movie out of – *BTS: Permission to Dance on Stage – LA*. Check it out!

"I can express my feelings and emotions in ways I can't in words through dance. The moment my body feels the music onstage is always exhilarating."

J-Hope excels at showing his art through movement.

The Boys are back! Hands up if you're excited.

WHAT TO EXPECT IN 2026

Get ready, ARMY! BTS's 2026 reunion tour is set to be the biggest, boldest and most bonkers world tour yet. Picture oceans of lightsticks, LED hearts and BT21 ears bouncing to the beat – from Jungkook's bunny brigade (yes, he's the rabbit prince!) to Jin's RJ alpaca caps. Add in bucket hats, glowing bracelets and purple heart wands, and you've got the global *event* of the decade. Only one unknown remains: will you be there?

BREAK THE STATES!

With their completely surprising breakthrough in America, BTS cemented themselves as big time superheroes. It was the stepping stones below that made their American dream come true ...

Seven Soulful Super Singers Smash the States – say that five times fast!

FIRST AMERICAN SHOWCASE

BTS made their US stage debut at KCON 2014 – America's largest K-Pop convention – in Los Angeles. They performed **'Boy in Luv'** and **'Danger'** before thousands of K-Pop fans. They were also the youngest act ever to perform on a bill that also included superstars G-Dragon and Girls' Generation. It was at this moment BTS also realised they were famous. "Thousands of fans were calling our name at the venue and almost everyone memorised the Korean lyrics," RM said. "Who would have thought people from across the ocean would love our songs? We were just grateful … and we still are."

The world belongs to BTS now – and we couldn't be happier about it.

UNITED STATES OF BTS

On 14th July, 2014, BTS stepped onto a US stage for their very first headline gig. Their surprise concert *Show & Prove,* at the Troubadour, West Hollywood, was planned with only two days' notice and filmed as a feature of their reality show *American Hustle Life*. They drew a sell-out crowd of 200 fans, with many more turned away due to the venue reaching capacity.

MIC DROP!

What happens when the world's most in-demand DJ teams up with the world's fastest-rising boy band? Future history, that's what! Steve Aoki's November 2017 remix of **'Mic Drop'** wasn't just a banger – it became BTS's first US Top 40 hit and the very first K-Pop track to top the American iTunes chart. Fittingly, the anthem was inspired by President Barack Obama's iconic – and literal – mic drop at his final White House Correspondents' Dinner in 2016, as he infamously exclaimed: "Obama out!"

Where's your cake, Mr Aoki?

"When I dreamed of becoming an artist, I listened to pop and watched all the awards shows in the United States. Being successful and being a hit in the US is such an honour as an artist."

Suga isn't taking his success for granted.

America's ARMY got a super show at the SoFi Stadium in LA.

STADIUM TAKEOVER

As part of their *Permission to Dance on Stage* concert series, BTS played sold-out shows at Los Angeles' SoFi Stadium in November and December 2021 – their first in-person concerts since 2019. More than 200,000 fans filled the venue across four nights, with a global audience watching at home via livestream. The run set records as the biggest box office draw at a single venue in nearly a decade. "There's nothing like seeing a full crowd in a sold-out stadium concert," V said afterwards, celebrating their live return.

BTS + MTV + VMA = YES!

BTS lit up the iconic MTV Video Music Awards in New York on 31st August, 2020, performing **'Dynamite'** live for the very first time! They also won their first Moonmen trophies: Best Group, Best Pop, Best Choreography and Best K-Pop.

Check this performance out on YouTube – wow!

LIVE! TONIGHT! SOLD OUT!

BTS crashed American late-night TV for the very first time on *Jimmy Kimmel Live!* in November 2017, performing **'Mic Drop'** to a studio full of screaming fans.

The moment the group truly broke America.

AND THE GRAMMY GOES TO ...

BTS made history in February 2019 when they stepped onto the Grammy Awards stage as presenters – the first K-Pop group ever to do so. Dressed in sleek black tuxedos, they announced the winner for Best R&B Album, handing the award to H.E.R. For BTS, it was a surreal moment. "Growing up in South Korea, we always dreamed of being on the Grammys stage," said RM onstage. "Thank you to all our fans for making this dream come true ... and we'll be back!"

Will they be the first K-Pop group to win a Grammy? YES.

"The fact that we have had success in the United States is very meaningful in and of itself."

RM, on the importance of an overseas fanbase.

MEMBER SPOTLIGHT RM

Leader. Producer. Rap monster. Actual genius. God of Destruction (i.e. a little bit clumsy). RM is all of the above – and so much more! Born on September 12, 1994, RM's real name is Kim Namjoon, but as a member of ARMY, you can call him 'Joonie' ...

BROTHERS THAT SING

RM was the very first member of BTS! He was recruited by **Big Hit Entertainment** in 2010 after being scouted by local producer, Sleepy. When the fledgling group's sound shifted from a hip hop to an idol group, RM was the only trainee to remain and a new band was built around him! "I started BTS because I wanted to say something," he told *Dazed* magazine in 2017. "There was a message inside me and I wanted to spread it as music."

HEIGHT: 181cm / 5'11" (tallest member)

****

FAVE FOOD: Pork belly (Samgyeopsal-gui)

****

FAVE TV: K-Dramas (*Pachinko*)

FANCY A SPOT OF NAMJOONING?

Coined by the ARMY, 'Namjooning' is a guide to better living as inspired by the many hobbies enjoyed by RM, BTS's most culturally enlightened member. (Sorry, Jimin!) It involves finding calm and mindfulness through self-care activities, such as appreciating and collecting art, reading (check out RM's Book Club!), visiting museums, learning about culture and spending time in nature. Have you namjooned today?

RM didn't understand the hide and seek game ...

WITH A LITTLE HELP FROM MY FRIENDS

As a teen, RM learned English by watching the US sitcom *Friends* repeatedly. It helped him master English vocabulary and pronunciation, a fluency that led him to become the group's spokesperson for international interviews and award shows, as well as the de facto leader of the band.

Could RM's linguistic skills *be* any more perfect?

MIC DROP!

RM originally stood for Rap Monster to represent his burgeoning skills on the mic. However, in 2017, RM changed the meaning of his stage name to mean 'Real Me'. "I wanted to better communicate who I am in the future," he told fans.

"It's my official role to represent BTS to the world and it's been a chance for me to mature as a person, but, behind the scenes, I'm just one of seven members and I'm inspired by the others all the time. I get free life lessons from them all."

RM learns from his beloved BTS brothers.

BRAINS OF THE BAND?

RM has an IQ of 148 – a near-genius level IQ. Albert Einstein's was 150! During his formative days at Seoul's Apgujeong High School, he was among the top one per cent of students in Korea.

"Hey, RM, where's my mic?"

When RM stands up for us, we stand up for him.

YOLO SOLO

RM is the most prolific member of BTS with more than 200 songwriting credits to his name. He's also the most active away from the group. He's released three solo albums/mixtapes: *RM* (2015), the critically acclaimed playlist *Mono* (2018) and his first official solo album *Indigo* (2022) – named after his favourite colour.

We can't tear ourselves away from these boys.

ALBUM SPOTLIGHT

LOVE YOURSELF:

Released on 18th May, 2018, *Love Yourself: Tear* made history as the first album by Korean artists to smash the US Billboard chart to smithereens by going straight to No. 1, a pivotal moment that proved the Bangtan Boys not only ruled the world, but had changed it beyond all recognition.

LOVE AND LIES

The second instalment of the BTS concept album *Love Yourself* trilogy, *Tear* delves into the darker themes of love not explored by previous album, *Her*. It navigates the pain and sadness that comes from a love based on lies. The 11 tracks are arranged to tell a story from beginning to end, moving from a superficial kind of love to the painful emotions felt by loss, separation and self-doubt.

TEARS FOR FEARS

"The word 'Tear' in English is interesting," RM has said of why that word was chosen for the title. "You can shed tears and tear paper. The word symbolises what a break up means to each of us. It was tears for me, tearing apart for Suga. For J-Hope, it was fear of talking about after a break up. For Jimin, it was fear. Tear, tear and fear. These are three themes of how this album ends."

AOKI IS A-OK

BTS collaborated with Steve Aoki, the world's most successful DJ and record producer, in November 2017. Aoki first worked his trap-beat magic on the group's song **'Mic Drop'**, from the *Love Yourself: Her* sessions. BTS worked with Aoki again for *Tear*, producing track three, **'The Truth Untold'**, an epic piano ballad. The collaboration helped propel *Tear* to even greater success than its predecessor.

TEAR

PLAY IT AGAIN ...

1. Intro: Singularity
2. FAKE LOVE
3. The Truth Untold (feat. Steve Aoki)
4. 134340
5. Paradise
6. Love Maze
7. Magic Shop
8. Airplane pt.2
9. Anpanman
10. So What
11. Outro: Tear

We are secretly hoping that Jungkook's flowers are for us.

FAKE IT 'TIL YOU MAKE IT

'Fake Love' debuted at No. 10 on the US Billboard Hot 100 – the highest-charting song for a K-Pop group at the time. The song made its TV debut on 20th May, 2018, when BTS performed live at the 2018 Billboard Music Awards, the first time a Korean music act performed (and won!) there. It was the fastest K-Pop MV to hit 100 million likes on YouTube!

THE FIRST GRAMMY NOM

Love Yourself: Tear won Album of the Year at both the 2018 Melon Music Awards and the Mnet Asian Music Awards. The album was also famously nominated at the 2019 Grammy Awards for Best Recording Package, the first K-Pop band in American music history to receive a nom!

We heart J-Hope and Jimin giving double hearts!

SUGA'S DREAMS

"Our goal ... is to be number one on the US Billboard 100," Suga said. "It is true I want us to have a number one in America, to go to the Grammys and to become the singers with the greatest influence in the world. It could not come true, if I didn't speak of these things out loud. But now that I have, I will try hard to make it happen!" Looks like Suga's manifesting worked!

BY THE NUMBERS

All BTS albums sell in big numbers, but *Tear* was different. It was their first album to rack up an astonishing 1.44 million in pre-orders alone, going on to sell 1.6 million copies in its first two weeks in Korea, becoming the bestselling album in the country's history at the time. Upon its release, the album also hit No. 1 on the Apple Music charts in more than 65 countries, selling over 3.5 million copies, the band's biggest hit so far.

BREAK THE SWEAT!

Do you have permission to dance? We hope so because you don't want to miss out on BTS's groundbreaking choreography, a key ingredient to their constant viral success on social media.

DO YOU KALGUNMU?

The most defining feature of BTS's dance choreography, 'Kalgunmu' literally translates to 'knife-like synchronisation'. It refers to the perfect precision of synchronised movements when seven members move as one. A prime example of 'Kalgunmu' can be seen in their **'ON'** MV. K-Pop idols undergo years of rigorous training to master this synchronisation, stamina and a wide range of dance techniques, often spending more than ten hours a day in practice on a single routine.

... You put your left arm in, your left arm out ...

LET'S DAEHYEONG!

Formations, or daehyeongs, are a crucial element of BTS' choreography too. The members move seamlessly through a wide array of dynamic patterns, from very complex geometric shapes to fluid lines and circles, without breaking a step. These ever-changing formations are used to create stunning stage visuals and an evolving narrative, highlighting different members at key moments. **'Black Swan'** is a beautiful example.

The band when they heard spaghetti was on the menu.

What are they pointing at? Do we care? Yes, yes we do ...

MAKING A POINT

A BTS dance routine's most memorable move, 'pointeu anmu', meaning Point Dance, is often the part of the song that goes super viral on social media. Movements such as the 'shoulder dance' in **'Go Go'**, or the jacket-ripping move in **'Fake Love'**, or the sleek mic drop in **'MIC Drop'**. These catchy, repetitive motions are designed to be instantly recognisable and easy for fans to replicate at live shows – and their TikTok dance battles!

Who knew BTS were pioneers of the chicken dance?!

J-Hope, Jimin and Jungkook are known as the 'dance line', with J-Hope as the dance leader. They are the most skilled dancers in the group and perform the challenging moves.

INTO THE MIX

Choreography is crazy important in BTS MVs as the band know that the ARMY will be copying the moves the minute the video is released. "When I get questions about why K-Pop is so popular; I always tell them K-Pop is a great mix of music, videos, visuals, choreography, social media and real-life," RM has said.

THE KILLING PART

A 'Killing Part' is a short and visually striking moment in a performance. It's meant to be the showstopper, the 'killer' moment in the routine. It can either be a difficult dance move (Jungkook's floorwork in **'Blood Sweat & Tears'**, for example) or a powerful vocal line (Jin in **'The Truth Untold'**). Remember, while a Point Dance is a type of Killing Part, a Killing Part is not always a Point Dance! Obvs.

ACTING WITH YOUR FACE

A critical element of any BTS dance performance! Facial expressions, or 'pyojeong yeongi' literally means 'facial acting'. It's a key part of an idol's training to master a range of expressions, from fierce to charismatic, cool to cute, to perfectly match the vibe of a song. In **'IDOL'**, for example, the members' expressions are playful and defiant, while in **'Spring Day'** they are raw and emotional. This attention to detail is what makes BTS's performances worthy of second, third, fourth viewings.

Pink hair and a heart shirt: V was Valentine's Day ready.

BACK TO CENTRE

The band member in the centre of the dance formation is typically the one singing or rapping at that moment in the song. The constant swapping of the centre member is a key element of BTS's choreography; it ensures that every member gets their moment in the spotlight during the song. It also allows the narrative of the song or video to be seen through each member with their individual style and personality.

"On Wednesdays we wear pink" ... apart from Jimin.

Shout-out to Son Sungdeuk, long-time choreographer for BTS on many of their most iconic early choreographies; Keone Madrid, creator of the group's most dynamic routines; and Sienna Lalau, who won an MTV VMA for Best Choreography for **'ON'**.

STRIKE A POSE: BTS'S BEST CHOREO

1. Dope **2.** Blood Sweat & Tears **3.** MIC Drop (Steve Aoki Remix) **4.** Spring Day **5.** Fake Love **6.** Idol **7.** Boy with Luv **8.** ON **9.** Dynamite **10.** Black Swan

BEGIN THE SHOWS!

Did you manage to get your hands on the most coveted ticket of the year? Millions of fans braved ticket queues for the most anticipated comeback tour ever ... will you be there?

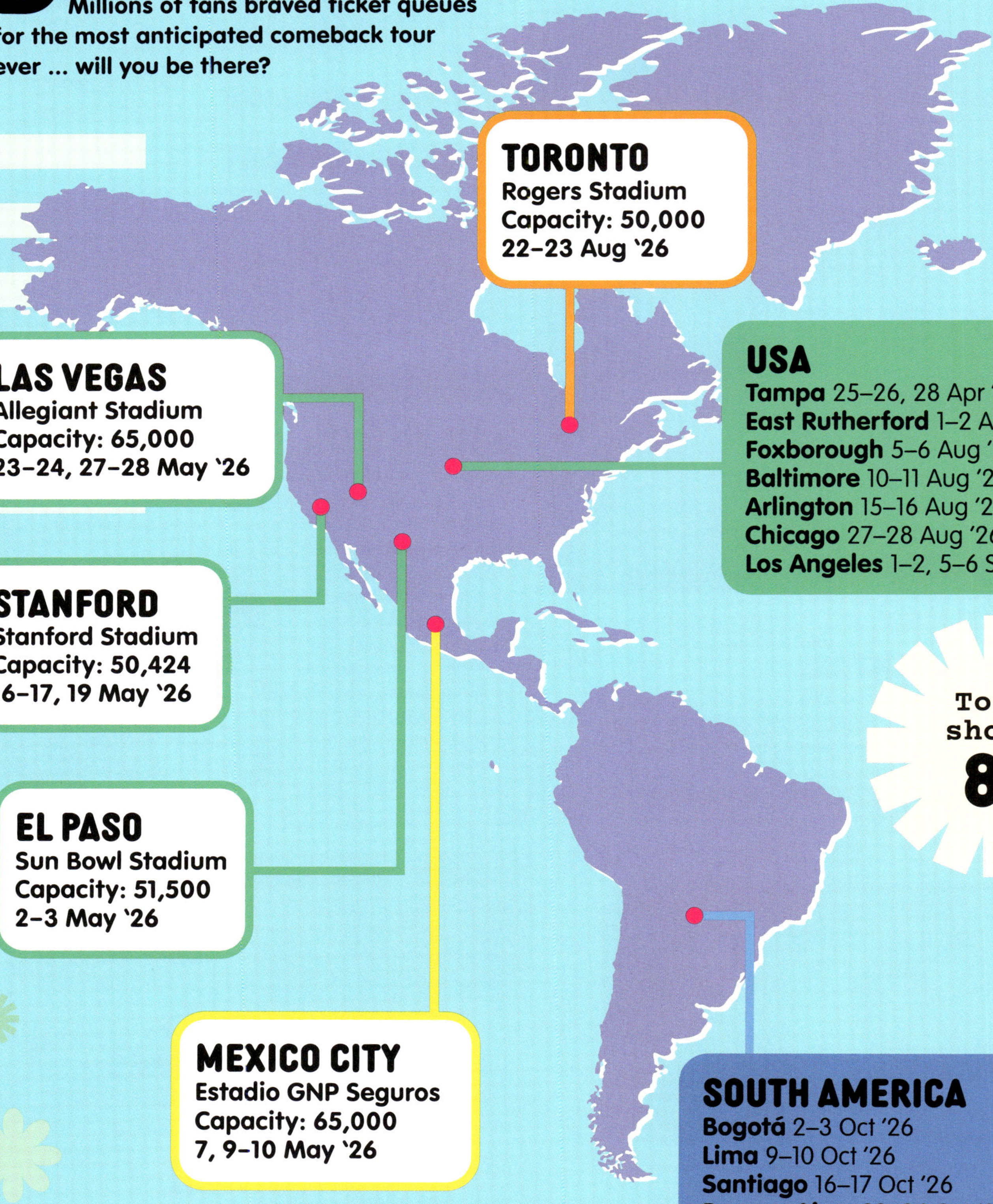

TORONTO
Rogers Stadium
Capacity: 50,000
22–23 Aug '26

LAS VEGAS
Allegiant Stadium
Capacity: 65,000
23–24, 27–28 May '26

USA
Tampa 25–26, 28 Apr '26
East Rutherford 1–2 Aug '26
Foxborough 5–6 Aug '26
Baltimore 10–11 Aug '26
Arlington 15–16 Aug '26
Chicago 27–28 Aug '26
Los Angeles 1–2, 5–6 Sept '26

STANFORD
Stanford Stadium
Capacity: 50,424
16–17, 19 May '26

Total shows:
82

EL PASO
Sun Bowl Stadium
Capacity: 51,500
2–3 May '26

MEXICO CITY
Estadio GNP Seguros
Capacity: 65,000
7, 9–10 May '26

SOUTH AMERICA
Bogotá 2–3 Oct '26
Lima 9–10 Oct '26
Santiago 16–17 Oct '26
Buenos Aires 23–24 Oct '26
São Paulo 28, 30–31 Oct '26

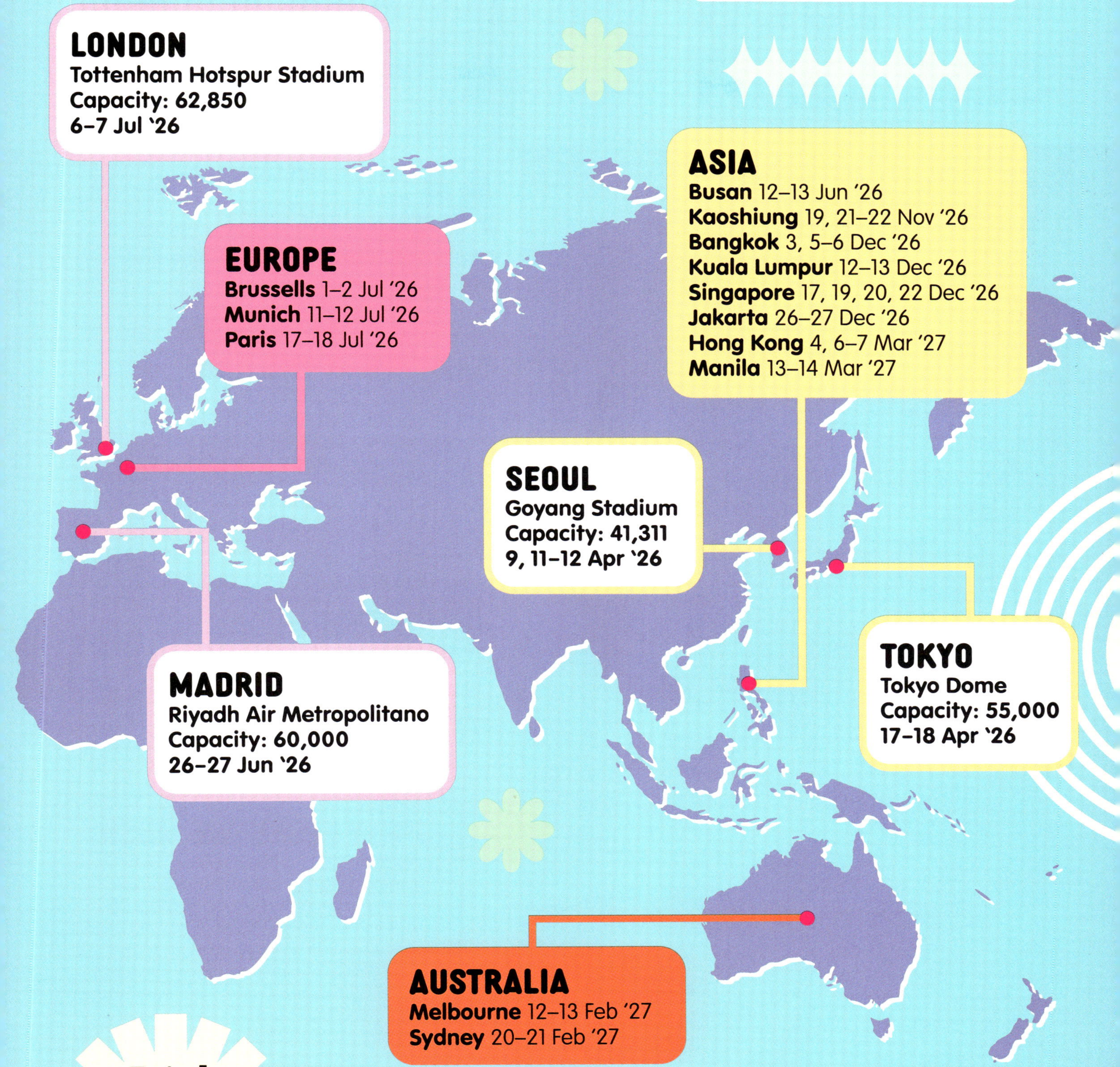

Total Countries Visited:
23

1272
Days since the last BTS concert

MEMBER SPOTLIGHT → JIMIN

Mochi. ChimChim. Jiminie. Chim Felon. Dooly. Baby J. Manggaetteok. Little Prince. All perfect nicknames for the one and only – Park Jimin!

DANCING IN THE RAIN

As a teenager at Busan High School of Arts, Jimin was a contemporary dance prodigy, inspired by K-Pop pioneer and dance sensation, Rain. Determined to follow in his idol's footsteps, he threw himself into his studies and quickly rose to the top of his class. To sharpen his skills, he also enrolled at Busan's Just Dance Academy, where he mastered modern styles such as popping, locking and hip hop.

JIMINONYM

Jimin stands among the world's great mononyms: Madonna, Kylie, Beyoncé, Prince. But things almost turned out differently. Before debut, he considered stage names such as 'Baby J', 'Baby G' or 'Young Kid' before sticking with his own name. "I decided that Jimin was the best!"

HEIGHT: 174cm / 5'9"

****

FAVE FOOD: Seafood

****

FAVE TV: *Attack on Titan*

JIMIN FACES THE MUSIC

In March 2023, Jimin released his debut solo album *Face*, a title that resonated on several levels. "The word 'face' has many different meanings," he said. "It has the meaning of the noun, face, but it also means, 'to confront,' as a verb. In order to begin a new journey, I thought it would be necessary to look back at myself and face myself entirely." The album debuted at No. 1 in South Korea and No. 2 on the US chart – the highest ever for a Korean solo artist!

Jimin speaks from the heart at the White House.

A face that only the ARMY could love – just kidding!

The slang term *delulu* – short for delusional – exploded in K-Pop fandoms and Jimin is often credited with popularising it. During a 2014 livestream, he jokingly used the word to describe fans' daydreams about their idols and it soon sparked endless memes. The ARMY quickly adopted it and the phrase spread into wider Internet culture!

THE KING OF K-POP?

Jimin has often been crowned the 'King of K-Pop' a title reinforced by his record-breaking solo success. In 2025, his track **'Who'** became the longest-charting K-Pop solo song on the US Billboard Hot 100, logging 32 weeks and surpassing Psy's 2012 global smash **'Gangnam Style'**. Fans have also supported Jimin's reign, crowning him on King Choice, the largest international K-Pop voting platform.

"Practice is the answer. If I have some time after I finish work in the evenings, I practice singing with the producers. I practice dancing. I keep trying to spend as much time practicing as I can. It's just an infinite cycle of practicing."

Jimin is dedicated to improving himself, if that's even possible!

THE LAST ONE TO JOIN

Jimin was the final member added to BTS – and he almost didn't make the cut! During his trainee days, he pushed himself to the limit, sometimes sleeping just two hours a night while practising until 4 am, before waking at 6 am to train again. After debut, Jimin revealed his training period was very short, just six months, the shortest of all the members.

LET'S GET CRAZY

With *Face*'s lead single **'Like Crazy'**, Jimin became the first Korean solo artist in history to top the US chart with a Korean-language song, setting a Guinness World Record in the process as the fastest K-Pop solo song to reach No. 1 in 100 countries. The song was inspired by a 2011 romantic drama of the same name, starring Felicity Jones and Anton Yelchin, a couple torn apart by distance.

A MESSAGE TO JIMIN FROM RYAN GOSLING ...

"Hi Jimin, it's Ryan Gosling here. I notice that your **'Permission to Dance'** *outfit is the same as my Ken outfit in the movie Barbie. I have to give it to you – you wore it first. You definitely wore it best and there's an unspoken Ken code that if you bite another Ken's style, you have to give them your most prized possession. I hope you'll accept Ken's guitar as my humble offering. Besides, Ken doesn't really play anyway, so... it'll be much better in your hands."*

In 2023, Hollywood heartthrob Ryan Gosling gifted Jimin the guitar his character Ken used in the billion-dollar-blockbuster movie, *Barbie*, as Jimin's **'Permission to Dance'** music video outfit served as inspiration for one of the iconic outfits Gosling wore for the role!

From one hearthrob to another!

ALBUM SPOTLIGHT

MAP OF THE SOUL:

The group's most personal album, *Map of the Soul: 7* celebrated the joy (and pain!) of being in a septet for seven years ...

SHADOW & EGO

Originally planned as a trilogy of albums named *Persona, Shadow and Ego,* the group merged the three concepts into an ambitious 20-track double album. They changed their approach after they took their first extended break in 2019 and came back feeling reenergised.

SEVEN YEAR FRIENDS

"I've seen these guys for the past seven years and sometimes I'm a little bit tired of them," said RM, during promotion for the album. As a result of the band's tight-knit professional and personal lives, *Map of the Soul: 7* became both a diary of the group's creative struggles and a celebration of their unity in the face of being one of the longest-surviving idol groups. The lyrics to the track **'Friends'** really sums up how Jimin and V feel about each other after all this time – and their infamous 'falling out over some dumplings' incident in 2016!

JUNG, CARL ... NOT KOOK

"*'Who am I?' is the question I've had all my life and I'll probably never find the answer*!" So raps RM on opening track, **'Intro: Persona'**. Carl Jung, the founding father of analytical psychology, was the first to develop theories of the Persona, Shadow and Ego – concepts that BTS explore here, inspired by the 1988 book *Jung's Map of the Soul*. RM later admitted none of the members read the book!

Classic J-Hope – always the prankster!

SOUTH KOREAN THRILLER

Upon its release in February 2020, *Map of the Soul: 7* set a Guinness World Record as South Korea's bestselling album ever, selling more than 4.8 million copies in just nine days! No K-Pop group has yet to beat that feat. But that's not all. It became 2020's bestselling album *in the whole world*!

SHEER ED-UCATION

For *Map of the Soul: Persona* (2019), BTS enlisted Ed Sheeran to co-write **'Make It Right'**, produced by rising UK talent Fred Again. "Ed actually sent us an email," RM revealed of the collab. "He just suddenly contacted us, with his songs. He said he had a present, like Santa Claus! And, that is just how that happened. Couldn't believe it!" The collab marked the first of two with Sheeran, the second being 2021's **'Permission to Dance'**. Despite the worldwide success together, RM later confessed to ARMY that the group had never met Ed – and still haven't!

Do you love BTS more than Ed? That's the question!

7

MAP OF THE SOUL: 7

1. Intro: Persona
2. Boy With Luv (feat. Halsey)
3. Make It Right
4. Jamais Vu
5. Dionysus
6. Interlude: Shadow
7. Black Swan
8. Filter
9. My Time
10. Louder than Bombs
11. ON
12. UGH!
13. 00:00 (Zero O'Clock)
14. Inner Child
15. Friends
16. Moon
17. Respect
18. We Are Bulletproof: The Eternal
19. Outro: Ego
20. ON (feat. Sia)

BLACK SWAN

The album's artistic showstopper, **'Black Swan'**, dives deep into what J-Hope described as "the fear we face as artists", the dreaded thought of losing the passion for their music. The track dropped first as an art film with the Slovenian MN Dance Company, instantly going viral for its beautiful choreography and bewitching visuals. Critics hail the video as a profound, experimental masterpiece.

CANCELLED

Before its release, the boys planned a *Map of the Soul* world tour to promote the album, but it was delayed and ultimately cancelled due to the COVID-19 pandemic. The *Map of the Soul Tour* was set to be their most ambitious stadium world tour yet, with more than 35 shows across 17 cities. Early ticket sales indicated it would break box office records, with millions of fans snapping up seats in record-breaking times.

BEYOND THE STUDIO

BTS are the busiest boy band on the planet. When they're not in the studio, they're out in the wild trying to save the world with these good deeds ...

ALL THE PRESIDENT'S MEN

From 2018 to 2022, BTS turned the United Nations (UN) stage in New York into their own stadium, giving speeches that spotlighted causes important to them. As South Korean President Moon Jae-in's 'Special Envoys for Future Generations and Culture', the band spoke on issues such as youth empowerment, self-love, mental health and climate change.

A SPECIAL INVITATION

On 31st May, 2022, BTS were invited to meet US President Joe Biden at the White House, in Washington, D.C! They were there to discuss Asian representation and anti-Asian hate crimes. The president praised the band: "People care a lot about what you say. It's not just your great talent, it's the message you're communicating. It *matters*." At the press briefing afterwards, V told the world's media: "We hope that today is one step closer to respecting and understanding each and every one as a valuable person." Well said.

BTS's eighth member – President Biden!

"Our generation studied English listening to pop songs, but now the global audience is learning Korean to understand BTS songs."

South Korea's First Lady, **Kim Jung-sook**

Proof that BTS are more than just pop stars.

LOVE UNICEF

BTS launched the 'Love Myself' campaign with United Nations Children's Fund (UNICEF) on 17th November, 2017 to help stop worldwide violence against children. At his inaugural UN assembly, RM said: "Tell me your story. I want to hear your voice and I want to hear your conviction. No matter who you are, where you're from, your skin colour, gender identity: speak yourself." The band then pledged a portion of the *Love Myself* album sales and concert proceeds to the campaign. To date, it's raised nearly $4 million!

Idols become icons! Making history once again.

"We have always wanted to be a positive influence in the world whether it may be through our music or our actions."

RM is basically a good human.

DANCING AT THE UNITED NATIONS

At the 2021 UN General Assembly, BTS spoke as South Korea's 'Special Presidential Envoys', urging young people to take action on climate change. "I hope we don't consider the future as grim darkness," Jungkook said solemnly. "There are still many pages left in the story about us!" To then ensure their message got maximum exposure, the boys premiered a unique **'Permission to Dance'** video, filmed inside the iconic UN Assembly Hall – the first time the venue had ever been used for a music video!

BURN THE STAGE

Released on YouTube Premium (and later as a film), BTS's eight-episode documentary *Burn the Stage* pulled back the curtain on BTS's 2017 *Wings* world tour to reveal not just the glamour of global tours, but the exhaustion, self-doubt and mental health struggles the band members all faced. It's a candid look inside the world's most famous group: "Our fans think we show our lives without filtering anything, but we hide a lot of things," Suga says in the show. "We showed our fans the raw side."

BTS as you've never seen them before – check it out!

Korea's national pride – well done, Boys!

HWAGWAN ORDER OF CULTURAL MERIT

In October 2018, BTS were awarded South Korea's Hwagwan Order of Cultural Merit. President Moon Jae-in gifted the group this prestigious honour, the highest in South Korea, for their role in spreading Korean culture worldwide. President Moon Jae-in (a dedicated ARMY member) praised the group: "BTS has greatly raised the national dignity by enhancing the stature of K-Pop and Korean culture and I am grateful in many ways."

BRIDGE THE SOUNDS

It must be true that BTS are the biggest and best band on the planet because their famous collaborators are equally as big and as brilliant, as this superstar line-up shows ...

TURN IT ON!

Australian pop star Sia joined BTS on **'ON'**, a stadium-ready anthem from 2020's *Map of the Soul: 7*. Her soaring soprano stitched seamlessly with the group's dynamite dynamic, elevating the track into a No. 4 hit on the US chart. The song's success was bolstered by BTS's iconic performance at New York's Grand Central Station on *The Tonight Show Starring Jimmy Fallon*, often voted the boys' best live TV appearance.

Take a bow, Sia!

ASIAN PRIDE

To celebrate BTS's first official all-English single, 2018's **'Waste It On Me'**, the group teamed up with superstar DJ Steve Aoki once again, following their smash collab **'MIC Drop'**. Its music video made headlines too for featuring an all-Asian cast of stars: Jamie Chung, Ken Jeong, Ross Butler and Aoki's sister, model Devon Aoki.

Him again – Steve loves the BTS Boys!

AMERICAN IDOL

American rapper Nicki Minaj's fiery remix verse – and an alternate MV – gave BTS's 2018 single **'IDOL'** a huge kick in the US. The original video, bursting with Korean heritage references from hanbok-inspired outfits to tiger imagery, smashed records with 45.9 million YouTube views in 24 hours. The choreography, blending traditional Korean movement motifs with modern hip hop energy, sparked the viral 'Idol Challenge' too, turning **'IDOL'** into a global dance craze!

"It's very special to me that the most popular artist in the world speaks Korean ... and it just feels very hopeful to me, in terms of thinking of the world as one family."

Coldplay front man, **Chris Martin** feels the BTS love.

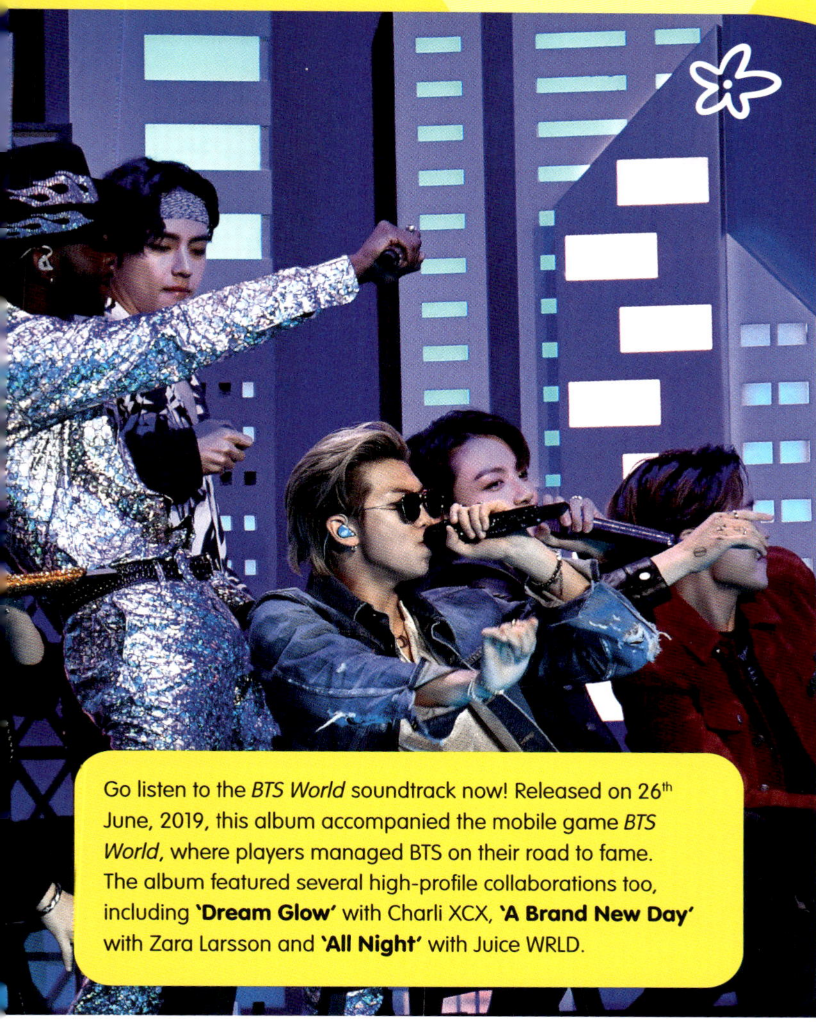

Go listen to the *BTS World* soundtrack now! Released on 26th June, 2019, this album accompanied the mobile game *BTS World*, where players managed BTS on their road to fame. The album featured several high-profile collaborations too, including **'Dream Glow'** with Charli XCX, **'A Brand New Day'** with Zara Larsson and **'All Night'** with Juice WRLD.

GOOD DECISIONS

Before enlisting for military service in 2022, BTS dropped one last extra-hot collab: **'Bad Decisions'** with uber-producer (and Selena Gomez's husband) Benny Blanco and 'America's Doggfather' Snoop Dogg. The single became their tenth Top 10 stateside hit! The playful music video was an instant fan favourite, starring Blanco as an over-the-top ARMY superfan preparing for a BTS concert – only to hilariously miss the show!

YOU ARE MY UNIVERSE

With more than 1.5 billion streams on Spotify and debuting at No. 1 on the US Billboard chart, BTS's collaboration with British rock group Coldplay in 2021 on **'My Universe'** was as surprising as it was special. It was BTS's first track released by two co-lead groups and was co-written by both bands. The song was acclaimed for showcasing bilingual lyrics and a clear mutual respect of each other's fan base. Surely another collab is on the cards?

Chris Martin is the world's No.1 BTS stan.

FUTURE HISTORY

When Psy, the 'father of K-Pop' (after **'Gangnam Style'** became the first global K-Pop hit in 2012) teamed up with BTS's Suga, it was like the past meeting the future. Their collaboration **'That That'**, released in April 2022, was co-written with Suga and is an absolute banger. The Wild West-themed MV was a viral sensation too, with its cowboy costumes only adding to Psy and Suga's playful horsey moves, that sparked memes and dance challenges on TikTok.

Have you ever done the horsey dance?

THE RIGHT MOMENT

Jungkook's collab with American singer-songwriter Charlie Puth on the hot hit, **'Left and Right'** easily surpassed one billion Spotify streams when it came out in 2022. Charlie was very impressed with his perfectly-pitched co-star: "It's very easy collaborating with Jungkook," Charlie said. "I had it in my head for a while that somebody would sing this song with me and I thought Jungkook would be perfect for it. We have this musical chemistry. He then sent over a *perfect* vocal."

'Left and Right' is such an amazing song.

MEMBER SPOTLIGHT → V

Kim Taehyung – or V as you know and love him – is the most-followed K-Pop idol on Earth. And he can prove it ...

SECRET WEAPON

Before their debut, V was considered BTS's 'secret weapon'. V was deliberately absent from pre-debut videos and teasers. The strategy was designed to showcase his striking visuals and vocal talent at the perfect moment – and prevent rival companies from trying to steal him!

LIFE THROUGH A LENS

On his days off, V dives into his other creative pleasures – art and photography. V even created an artistic alter ego, Vante, inspired by his favourite photographer Ante Badzim. He also paints and is inspired by the great master of art, Vincent Van Gogh.

HEIGHT: 179cm / 5'10"

****

FAVE FOOD:
Korean barbecue

****

FAVE TV:
Princess Hours and *Itaewon Class*

V was the most-searched K-Pop artist worldwide in 2024! Wow!

V on the hunt for a McFlurry – as always!

V – not to scale, obviously.

YOLO SOLO

8th September, 2023 saw V drop his debut album, *Layover*. It was a hot infusion of jazz, R&B and synth-pop. In South Korea, the album sold more than 1.6 million copies on day one, the highest first-day sales ever for a solo K-Pop artist!

V was allowed to pick his own stage name, with Big Hit suggesting either Lex or Six. "The members all said that V fit me the best and so I picked V … to stand for victory!"

"I lived in the countryside so I didn't imagine doing anything except for farming in the future. That changed after I fell in love with music."

The power of music has changed **V**'s life.

PURPLE POWER

Borahae! V's now-iconic phrase – "I purple you!" in English – was coined at a fan meeting in November 2016. The phrase is short for "I'll trust and love you for a long time." Since then, purple has become ARMY's symbolic colour worldwide. The top of New York's iconic Empire State Building was even illuminated purple in 2019 to honour BTS during the group's visit to New York. Purple is a colour historically associated with royalty – just sayin'!

The group's self-proclaimed "good boy". Do you agree?

ACCLAIMED ACTOR

Being in BTS is not quite enough for Mr V. In 2016, he debuted as an actor under his real name, Kim Taehyung, in the historical K-drama *Hwarang: The Poet Warrior Youth*. V played Hansung, a young student of the elite warrior class. SPOILER ALERT: In the drama's most emotional moment, Hansung sacrifices himself to protect his friends. His death was heartbreaking for ARMY!

AN ACCIDENT WAITING TO HAPPEN

V joined BTS by accident in 2011. He went to support a friend who was auditioning, but staff at Big Hit urged him to try out as well. At first he wasn't sure: "I called my dad and asked for his permission to audition. I thought I would fail for sure, but then they contacted me saying I passed. I thought it was a lie! I was the only one to pass that day." Imagine V not in BTS – actually don't, it's utterly unthinkable!

INSTAGRAM MAN

In December 2021, each member of BTS launched their own Instagram account – and V instantly made history. Within hours, he had broken two Guinness World Records: fastest to one million followers (43 minutes) and fastest to ten million (four hours, 52 minutes). Today, V is the most-followed K-Pop idol on Instagram, with more than 70 million followers – and counting!

ALBUM SPOTLIGHT

BE

An injection of upbeat pop that made our legs dance and our mouths sing, *Be* was the ideal antidote for the planet as it recovered from the pandemic ...

BE

1. Life Goes On
2. Fly to My Room
3. Blue & Grey
4. Skit
5. Telepathy
6. Dis-ease
7. Stay
8. Dynamite

BE HERE NOW

November 2020 marked the release of *Be*, just nine months after *Map of the Soul: 7*. Created in lockdown at Big Hit's Seoul studio, the album was BTS's direct response to the world shutting down. The band wanted to comfort ARMY through this frightening time, so they lived together in their own bubble to record.

A THOUGHT FROM JIN ...

"We tried to honestly express the emotions we feel right now on *Be*. This album is like a page in our diary of the times we are currently living in. The album title *'BE'* represents 'being'." Jin hoped that the album would bring comfort to their fans during uncertain times.

LIFE GOES ON

'Life Goes On' became the group's first non-English song to debut at No. 1 on the US chart and the first Korean song to ever hit the top spot in America! The MV – the first and only one directed by Jungkook so far – has become as iconic as the song. It follows V driving through quiet streets before cutting to the members lounging around, playing games, watching movies and making music. It climaxes with the band performing to an empty stadium! "The message is simple – life goes on," RM said.

There's always one, isn't there?

DRESSED FOR SUCCESS

BE debuted at No. 1 in more than 20 countries! A large part of this success is down to many of the group's several live performances of the lead single **'Life Goes On'**, featuring them dressed in nothing but pyjamas and bathrobes! Don't believe us? Check out their iconic performance on *Good Morning America* in November 2020. It's got 33 million views!

THE RETURN OF THE SKIT

Every BTS album once featured a 'skit', a casual conversation captured mid-album between the band. With *Be*, the band revived the tradition for the first time since 2017's *Love Yourself: Her*. They had good reason: they celebrated **'Dynamite'** hitting No. 1 on the US chart. "The Billboard No. 1 artist has entered!" Jin laughed as he introduced the track. Fittingly, the skit was recorded on Jungkook's birthday too and fans can hear his mix of disbelief and joy: "The best birthday present ever is Billboard No. 1!" he said.

"We would have been on a world tour if it had not been for the pandemic. As a result, we were able to release **'Dynamite'** and reach the top of the Billboard Hot 100. Through the many ups and downs we realised that 'life goes on', which is the message we wanted to deliver through *Be*."

J-Hope

J-HOPE'S MESSAGE OF HOPE

"We started *Be* by getting together and asking what kind of story we wanted to tell. The end result of that conversation was, 'Well, hey, we still have to live with this situation; we can't give up.' And from there, **'Life Goes On'** was born and then we got to work on the stories we each wanted to tell. I think *Be* sounds more raw." J-Hope explained that the album tried to capture the emotions everyone felt living through the covid pandemic.

HOMEMADE

For *Be*'s promotional photos that showcase the album's theme, each member designed a set modelled after their own bedroom. RM's room was filled with books and sculptures; Jin's glowed in bright pastels; Suga kept his minimalist; J-Hope's burst with plants; Jimin's was soft and snuggly; Jungkook's was littered with recording equipment; V's resembled an art gallery. ARMY loved how the rooms mirrored their personalities … and enjoyed the sneak-peek into their bedrooms, too!

RM thanks the ARMY at the AMA's.

BEYOND THE STARS

BTS have collected more than 500 major awards, proof that you can't spell BEST without B, T and S! Their trophy shelf is buckling under the weight of their awesomeness, with career-defining wins like these ...

THE X FACTOR

Back in 2015, BTS may have been rookies, but they were already bulletproof. That year they won South Korea's Golden Tweet for a group selfie snapped after the Melon Music Awards. With three million retweets, it became the most retweeted post of the year. To celebrate, Twitter (now X) honoured them with a special emoji: a tiny bulletproof-vest logo. It was the first time a K-Pop group ever received a personalised emoji!

Can you tell who's taking the selfie?

SUPERHOT WINNING STREAK

At the height of their first ascension to become global superstars, BTS achieved a feat not awarded since The Beatles in the 1960s: four US No. 1 albums in under two years. The winning streak began with *Love Yourself: Tear* (June 2018), *Love Yourself: Answer* (September 2018), *Map of the Soul: Persona* (April 2019) and *Map of the Soul: 7* (March 2020). And the streak didn't stop there: their next two releases, *Be* (November 2020) and *Proof* (June 2022) also debuted at No. 1.

Sorry, Justin! You got beat by BTS!

BEATING BIEBER

"If anyone knows how to make history, it's BTS!" So said Justin Bieber in 2020. And he should know. He was trounced by them in 2021 and 2022 when they held the No. 1 spot on the US Billboard's Social 50 chart for an unprecedented *210 consecutive weeks*, breaking Bieber's previous record of 164. To date, no artist has beaten this extraordinary run!

"Who would've thought we could win artist of the year at an American awards ceremony? It was so shocking. It sent chills down my spine."

Jung Kook was excited to be recognised by the AMAs.

RUN BTS RUN!

To thank the group for announcing the title of their 2026 album, *Arirang*, in January 2026 – news that once again broke the Internet – ARMY propelled **'Run BTS'** to No. 1 on both the World Digital Song Sales chart and the U.S. Billboard chart for the first time. Sales of the song surged by a whopping 18,000 per cent! Originally released in June 2022 just ahead of the group's military service, the track supported their anthology album *Proof* and has long been a fan favourite.

Artist of the Year at the 2021 American Music Awards!

MAKING HISTORY – AGAIN!

The Billboard Music Awards is America's most prestigious awards show. And, as of 2022, BTS hold the record as the most-awarded K-Pop group with 12 wins. Their haul includes five consecutive Top Social Artist trophies (2017–2021), Top Song Sales Artist, Top Duo/Group and Top Selling Song for **'Butter'**. It's of little surprise: the awards are fan-voted and no fandom is louder than ARMY.

Putting South Korea on the global pop map!

AMERICAN DREAM

At the American Music Awards, 2019, BTS became the first K-Pop group to ever win an award: Favourite Group. Two years later, in 2021, they even won Artist of the Year, another historic first for a K-Pop act. The group were grateful: "The AMAs are the most American of award ceremonies and an almost equal authority to the Grammys," RM said. "I greatly felt that instead of introducing us at the ceremony as some exotic kids from Asia, they respected and welcomed us as just another part of the show."

The Boys are looking good as gold!

NOM NOM NOM NOM NOM

In 2021, BTS became the first K-Pop act to receive a Grammy Award nomination for Best Pop Duo/Group Performance for **'Dynamite'**. It was a huge deal: Grammys are the most desired music award! BTS followed with four more nominations, though each time losing out to stars such as Lady Gaga, Ariana Grande, Doja Cat and SZA. "I grew up watching the Grammys," Suga said. With their new album, BTS are Grammy favourites for 2027.

This was a moment that changed pop music forever!

BIG TIME SUCCESS

Shattering records and collecting countless awards comes as standard with BTS. They've smashed an extraordinary stack of statistics to prove they're No. 1, by being anything but by-the-numbers, as these MASSIVE figures show ...

We're over here, Boys!

ONE IN THIRTEEN

This is crazy! In 2020, the Hyundai Research Institute (HRI) revealed that 800,000 visitors travel to South Korea every year because of BTS. The survey estimated that one in every 13 visitors was on a BTS-inspired pilgrimage, from exploring the members' hometowns to stopping at Big Hit's original building in Seoul, HYBE's Insight Museum, favourite cafés of the group and murals of the band in Busan and Daegu.

Hands up who fancies a trip to South Korea?

V IS FOR VICTORY!

BTS's official Instagram account (@bts.bighitofficial) has more than 77.5 million followers, as of October 2025. That's the population of the UK! This staggering stat makes them the most followed pop group in the world and earned them the Guinness World Record to prove it.

From January 2013 to December 2022, BTS dominated social media with more than two billion mentions – that's more than 550,000 every day! And it wasn't just a handful of superfans: 40 million unique users worldwide posted about BTS.

Murals of the group have sprung up all over South Korea.

BIG HIT BUSINESS

The boys' success back in South Korea generates MASSIVE amounts of cash for the country's economy, roughly $4.9 billion annually, according to the Korea Culture and Tourism Institute. This equates to more than 5.5 trillion won in Korea's currency. Even more staggering is that after the boys' mandatory military service was announced, Big Hit (now known as HYBE) saw a 40 per cent *decrease* in profits due to the group's inactivity.

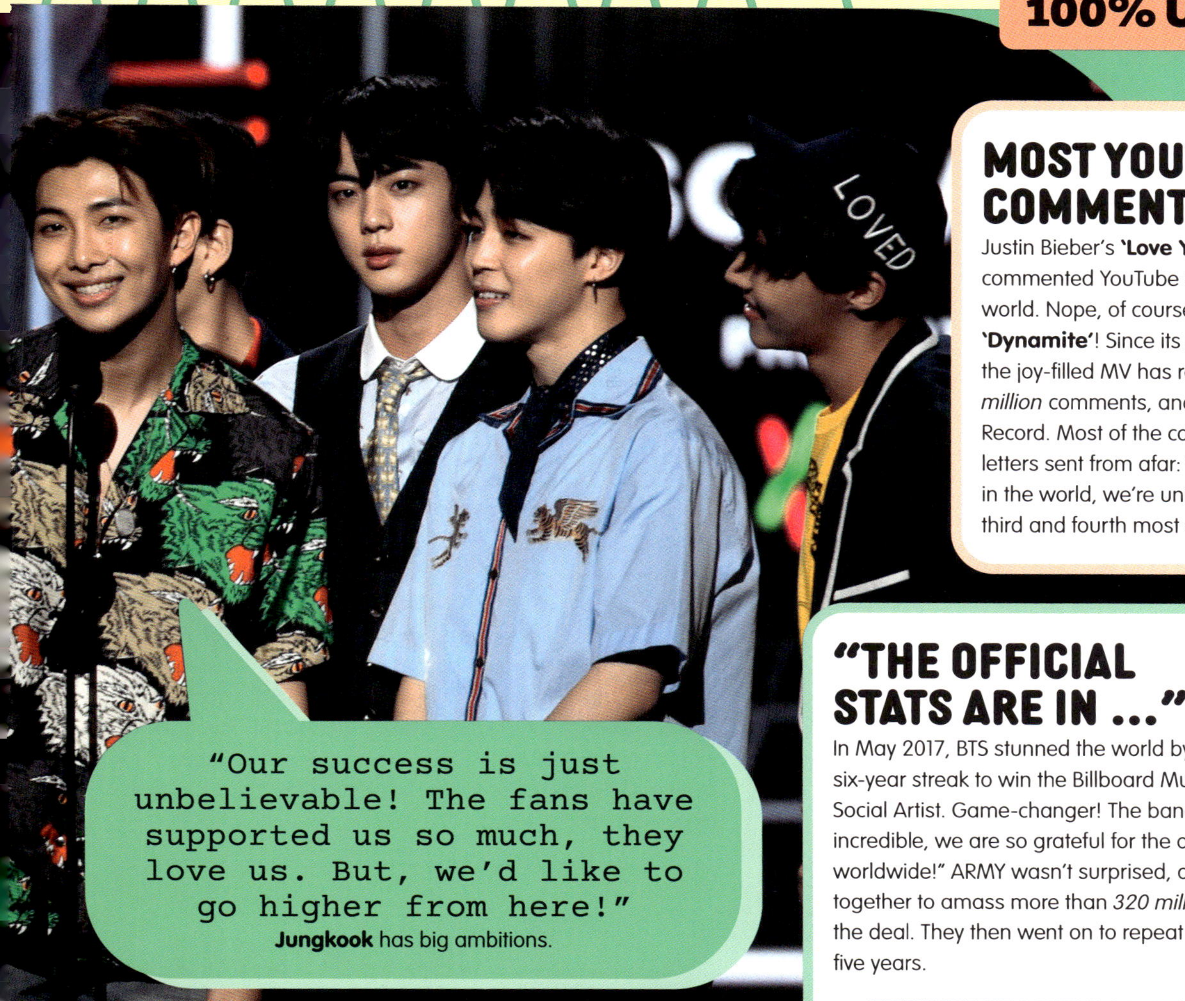

> "Our success is just unbelievable! The fans have supported us so much, they love us. But, we'd like to go higher from here!"
> **Jungkook** has big ambitions.

MOST YOUTUBE COMMENTS – EVER!

Justin Bieber's **'Love Yourself'** is the most commented YouTube music video in the world. Nope, of course it's not, silly – it's BTS's **'Dynamite'**! Since its release in August 2020, the joy-filled MV has racked up more than *16 million* comments, another Guinness World Record. Most of the comments read like love letters sent from afar: "No matter where we are in the world, we're united for BTS!" The second, third and fourth most commented MV? Also BTS!

"THE OFFICIAL STATS ARE IN ..."

In May 2017, BTS stunned the world by smashing Justin Bieber's six-year streak to win the Billboard Music Award for Top Social Artist. Game-changer! The band was amazed: "This is incredible, we are so grateful for the attention we are getting worldwide!" ARMY wasn't surprised, of course, they rallied together to amass more than *320 million* #BBMA votes to seal the deal. They then went on to repeat the feat for BTS for the next five years.

2027 will be the year BTS win BIG!

BEATING THE BEATLES

For decades, The Beatles (who, fun fact, also have a B, T and S in their name!) have reigned as the biggest-selling male pop group of all time. But BTS are hot on their heels! In 2025, it was revealed that BTS have sold a staggering *846 million* units worldwide across albums, singles and streams. That makes them the bestselling Asian act ever! This accomplishment was recognised by the IFPI who awarded BTS the Global Recording Artist of the Year trophy in 2021 and 2022. Watch out, Beatles!

Beatlemania took over the world in the 1960s.

BTS: STILL THE BEST

In a 2023 survey by South Korea's Ministry of Culture, BTS proved their superpower: 29 per cent of respondents across dozens of countries named them their favourite K-Pop act. The annual poll, which surveys fans aged 15–59, crowned BTS again in 2025 with 25 per cent, keeping them at the top spot. Remarkably, they maintained the top spot despite being inactive for three years during their military service.

MEMBER SPOTLIGHT → JUNG KOOK

*BIAS = favourite member!

HEIGHT: 178cm / 5'10"

****

FAVE FOOD: Pork belly, sashimi and ramen

****

FAVE TV: *Attack on Titan* and *Naruto*

As the group's Golden *Maknae*, Jungkook is often considered the band's bias,* because he's so cute and sweet and talented. It's no surprise ARMY calls him 'Kookie'!

WE HAVE RM TO THANK

In 2011, aged 14, Jungkook auditioned for *Superstar K3*, a South Korean television talent show series similar to *American Idol*. He was rejected. However, afterwards he received casting offers from several entertainment agencies, but he chose Big Hit Entertainment, for one simple reason: "I just simply thought RM was really cool!" he said. "When I saw him rap, I just thought he was really, really awesome. I believe maybe it was fate that drew me to him."

FOREVER YOUNG

Jungkook may be the *maknae* – the youngest – but he still excels at everything he puts his mind to: singing, rapping, dancing, sports and even art. It's no doubt down to Jungkook being influenced by other global teen prodigies, including Justin Bieber, Justin Timberlake and Usher. A Jungkook and JB collab will happen soon – watch this space!

Remember when Jungkook soared high above 60,000 fans at London's Wembley Stadium during the *Love Yourself* world stadium tour in 2019? His solo performance of **'Euphoria'** remains the most replayed concert visual in ARMY history!

Where Jungkook belongs – on the stage!

This kid became the biggest idol in the world!

JUNGKOOK'S GOLDEN CLOSET

Jungkook loves stepping behind the camera to direct. Not only did he direct the MV for **'Life Goes On',** he also directed short travel documentaries of the group. Armed with his own camera, he films the members exploring different cities, then edits the footage with hand-picked music. At just a few minutes long, these mini travelogues give ARMY an intimate glimpse into life on the road – and hint at Jungkook's passion for future filmmaking endeavours.

KOOKIE MONSTER

When the group individually launched their own Instagram accounts on the same day – 6th December, 2021, Jungkook gained 50 million followers, the most of the group. A year later, he deleted his account because he never used it. However, in July 2025, he opened a new Insta account and gained 7.1 million followers IN A DAY.

"We're extremely proud of what we've achieved, but we remember to never lose sight of the reason why we all started this journey. Performing and making music is everything to us and we hope to continue to spread our message this way even through all our successes."

Jungkook will never let fame go to his head!

Time to shine again, Kookie.

FIRST, LAST AND ONLY

In 2025, Jungkook was crowned the world's most favourite male K-Pop idol in a poll of 94 countries. That's nothing though. Between 2019 and 2022, he reigned as the most searched male K-Pop idol on Google – beating V to pole position. When Jungkook completed his military service in June 2025, the hashtag #JUNGKOOKISCOMINGBACK became the No. 1 social trend worldwide!

LUCKY NUMBER SEVEN

In July 2023, Jungkook released his first solo single, **'Seven'**. The track set a Guinness World Record as the fastest song to hit one billion Spotify streams – in just 108 days. Amazingly, it was originally written for Jungkook's idol, Justin Bieber! Grammy-winning songwriter Andrew Watt declared: "**'Seven'** could be the biggest song in the world if Jungkook sings it." He was right!

WORLD CUP

Cast your mind back to November 2022, if you can. It was the time when Jungkook became the first South Korean artist to release and perform an official FIFA World Cup soundtrack with the song '**Dreamers**'. More than 50 million fans tuned in. "Singing the World Cup Song, my voice will be recorded in the World Cup history – it's a huge honour," he said.

BILLION TOTAL STREAMS

With more than 45 *billion* – with a B! – total streams on Spotify, BTS are far and away the most in-demand pop group in the world. Welcome to the big time success ...

BILLION-STREAM BLOW-UP

'Dynamite' is BTS's most streamed song – so far, at least! Its two billion streams (!) makes total sense: it was the group's first fully English single, released in August 2020, at the height of the pandemic. The world needed this pop anthem to cheer it up! And it did just that. The track was also the first K-Pop song EVER to debut at No. 1 on the US Billboard chart. "In a way, that's almost frightening!" RM said of the monster success.

"With seven members we have seven different tastes. So when it comes to songwriting, it's like a big competition!"

RM gives us an insight into the seven-way writing process.

SMOOTH LIKE BUTTER

Do the boogie! Released on 21st May, 2021, **'Butter'** became BTS's second single to join the boys' 'billion club', as well as hit the top spot on the US Billboard charts – where it stayed for a record-breaking ten weeks! The song also set Spotify's record for the most-streamed song in its first 24 hours, with 11 million streams. Today, it has more than 1.5 billion streams on Spotify and one billion views on YouTube. Superstar glow, indeed!

Ain't no other – Hi Jin!

SO SICK!

The lead single from *Love Yourself: Tear*, **'Fake Love'** catapulted BTS into the big leagues when it came out on 18th May, 2018: it debuted at No. 10 on the US Billboard charts, making it BTS's first ever US Top 10 hit – they've now had more than ten! Despite its dark lyrical themes about love's devilish deception, the track also became the band's fifth 'billion club' entry in August 2025. The MV is particularly handsome too!

WHO DOES JIMIN THINK HE IS?

In July 2024, Jimin gave ARMY the world, when he released **'Who'**, the lead single from his second solo album, *Muse*. The track pushed Jimin to become the first Bangtan Boy to hit more than two billion streams on Spotify for solo work. Jimin will forever stand tall as the first Korean solo artist ever to top the US charts.

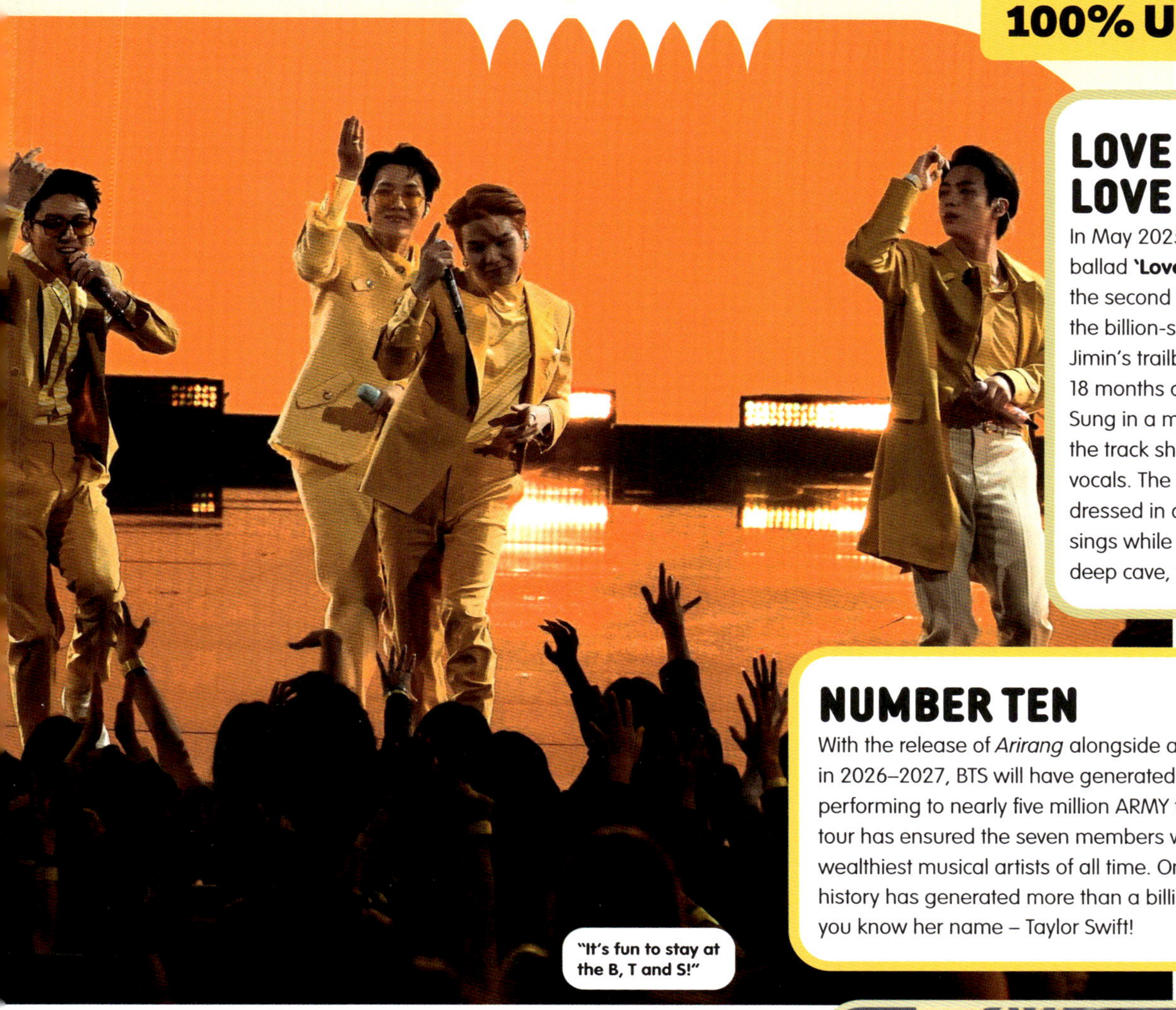

"It's fun to stay at the B, T and S!"

LOVE ME LOVE ME

In May 2025, with the soulful ballad **'Love Me Again'** V became the second BTS member to cross the billion-streams mark, following Jimin's trailblazing success – just 18 months after the song's release. Sung in a mix of Korean and English, the track showcases V's deep, velvety vocals. The MV is awesome too: V, dressed in a sparkly sequined top, sings while stuck at the bottom of a deep cave, filmed in Mallorca, Spain.

NUMBER TEN

With the release of *Arirang* alongside an 82-date world tour in 2026–2027, BTS will have generated more than $1 billion performing to nearly five million ARMY fans worldwide. The tour has ensured the seven members will become among the wealthiest musical artists of all time. Only one other artist in history has generated more than a billion dollars for a tour. Yes, you know her name – Taylor Swift!

'Dynamite' was so explosive that Spotify reported a 300 per cent spike in unique listeners on the group's channel after the song came out!

It's official, 'Boy with Luv' is a total banger!

TOTALLY IN LUV

"I would work with them again one hundred thousand times!" So said American singer-songwriter sensation Halsey after she collaborated with the boys back on 2019's **'Boy With Luv'** – the first ever Korean-language song to hit one billion Spotify streams! Halsey later gushed about BTS to *Time* magazine: "Behind those three letters are seven astounding young men who believe that music is stronger than the barriers of language." YES.

BTS'S BEST SONGS*

1. Blood Sweat and Tears
2. I Need U
3. Black Swan
4. Run
5. Save Me
6. Butterfly
7. Pied Piper
8. Not Today
9. Dimple (Illegal)
10. Spring Day

*As ranked by Billboard, July 2023.

BE THE SPARK

With BTS's success, the world has gone crazy for all things K-Pop! With the group's comeback in 2026, make sure you know these essential Korean terms ... just in case you ever spark up a conversation with them! You never know – it could happen!

ANNYEONGHASEYO (안녕하세요) *Ahn-nyeong-hah-seh-yo*

Hello. Be cool, just say *Ahn-nyeong.*

SARANGHAE (사랑해) *Sah-rahng-heh*

I love you.
Essential in case you ever get to speak to Jung Kook!

HWAITING (화이팅) *Hway-ting*

Good luck.
Something to shout as they walk on stage at their next concert.

DAEBAK (대박) *Deh-bahk*

Awesome.
The only way to describe Jimin. Even in the mornings.

MEOSITTA (멋있다) *Muh-shee-tta*

Handsome. Perfect for Mr Worldwide Handsome: Jin!

AMI (아미) *Ah-mee*

ARMY. This one is self-explanatory!

A double high five with Jung Kook!

"Whatever emotions I may be feeling, I'm always ready to express them."
Suga encourages others to be emotionally true to themselves.

RM talking about his love of crabs – again!

Did you know, in 2020, BTS launched the educational WeVerse series *Learn Korean With BTS* to help international fans engage more deeply with their music and content during the COVID-19 pandemic. The fun three-minute lessons were a hit, attracting more than two million viewers across 200 countries! *Daebak!*

GWIYEOWO (귀여워!) *Gwee-yuh-woh*
So cute. Suga, this one's for you!

CHINGU (친구) *Cheen-goo*
Friend. Because BTS are BFFs!

CHOEGO (최고) *Chweh-go*
The best.
The boys haven't been anything less than the best since 2013.

SELCA (셀카) *Sell-kah*
Selfie.
Essential, in case you see V gliding towards you. Imagine!

JJANG (짱) *Jjahng*
Supercool. All together now – *Bangtan jjang!*

MASHISSEO (맛있어) *Mah-shee-ssuh*
Delicious.
Just in case you taste some of Jin's famous ramen.

GEUMJJOK-I (금쪽이) *Geum-jjok-ee*
Precious one, or Golden Child.
ARMY use it to describe their bias, or favourite BTS member.

JOA (좋아) *Joh-ah*
I like it.
The only thing to say when Jimin debuts a new hair colour.

PICTURE CREDITS

FRONT COVER: PICTURES: Getty Images
5: PICTURES: Alamy Images, Sipa US/PictureGroup
6-7: PICTURES: Alamy Images, Abaca Press / Alamy Images, Associated Press, Rob Grabowski / Alamy Images, Everett Collection / Alamy Images, Top Photo Corporation / Alamy Images, Associated Press, Lee Jin-man
8-9 WORDS: WeVerse.io: BTS, 1 July 2025, Billboard.com: Mitchell Peters
PICTURES: Alamy Images, Newscom, BJ Warnick / Alamy Images, Yonhap/Newcom/Alamy Live News / Alamy Images, AP Photo/Luca Bruno / Alamy Images, Trafalgar Releasing / Courtesy Everett Collection / Alamy Images, AP Photo/Craig Ruttle / Alamy Images, Trafalgar Releasing / Courtesy Everett Collection
10-11: WORDS: X.com: @BTS, 17 December 2012, Elle.com: Alyssa Bailey
PICTURES: Alamy Images, Richard Brian/Sipa USA / Alamy Images, Lee Jae-Won/AFLO/Alamy Live News / Shutterstock, Kim Hee-Chul/EPA / Shutterstock, Jamie Lamor Thompson
12-13: WORDS: NME.com: Gladys Yeo, EW.com: Leah Greenblatt, Time.com: Raisa Bruner, New Yorker: Alex Barasch
PICTURES: Shutterstock, Seokyong Lee/Penta Press / Alamy Images, Newscom/Alamy Live News
14-15: WORDS: Rolling Stone.com: Brian Hiatt, *The Tonight Show Starring Jimmy Fallon:* Jimmy Fallon, Esquire.com: Dave Holmes
PICTURES: Shutterstock, Seokyong Lee/Penta Press / Shutterstock, Silvia Elizabeth Pangaro
16-17: WORDS: Rolling Stone.com: Brian Hiatt,
PICTURES: Alamy Images, ArcadeImages / Alamy Images, AP Photo/Lee Jin-man / Alamy Images, Aflo Co.Ltd/Nippon News / Alamy Images, Abaca Press/Alamy Live News / Alamy Images, Andrii Shevchuk
18-19: WORDS: BTS-trans.Tumblr.com, 24 August 2014, MBN Star, Vogue.sg: Alli Sim
PICTURES: Alamy Images, AP Photo/Kin Cheung / Shutterstock, Kim Hee-Chul/EPA
20-21: WORDS: RollingStoneIndia.com: Riddhi Chakraborty, Billboard.com: E Alex Jung, Eonline.com: Billy Nilles
PICTURES: Alamy Images, Trafalgar Releasing / Courtesy Everett Collection / Alamy Images, Sipa US/PictureGroup / Alamy Images, Frank Micelotta/PictureGroup / Shutterstock, Everett Collection / Shutterstock, Featureflash Photo Agency
22-23: WORDS: Vogue.com: Monica Kim
PICTURES: Shutterstock, Seokyong Lee/Penta Press / Alamy Images, Lee Jae-Won/AFLO/Alamy Live News / Alamy Images, Imaginechina Limited / Alamy Images, Conor Duffy/Sipa USA / Alamy Images, AP Photo/Chris Pizzello / Alamy Images, AP Photo/Ahn Young-joon / Shutterstock, Kim Hee-Chul/EPA / Alamy Images, Media Punch
24-25: WORDS: NME.com: Nick Reilly, *The Tonight Show Starring Jimmy Fallon:* Jimmy Fallon, 1 May 2023, Billboard.com: E Alex Jung, ktaebwi.tumblr.com: Star Naver
PICTURES: Alamy Images, Media Punch / Shutterstock, Capture Pix / Shutterstock, Seokyong Lee/Penta Press / Alamy Images, Sipa US / Shutterstock, Everett Collection / Shutterstock, Featureflash Photo Agency
26-27: WORDS: Rolling Stone.com: Brian Hiatt, Grammy.com: John Ochoa
PICTURES: Shutterstock, Broadimage / Shutterstock, YONHAP/EPA-EFE / Shutterstock, Yonhap/EPA / Shutterstock, Kathy Hutchins
28-29: PICTURES: Alamy Images, Scott Roth/Invision/AP / Alamy Images, ZUMA Press, Inc./Alamy Live News / Alamy Images, Aflo Co.Ltd/Nippon News / Alamy Images, Newscom/Alamy Live News / Alamy Images, Ben Hider/Invision/AP / Shutterstock, Sagase48 / Shutterstock, Dutchmen Photography
30-31: WORDS: NME.com: Rhiann Daly, New York Times: Andrew Russeth
PICTURES: Shutterstock, Kim Hee-Chul/EPA / Alamy Images, UPI/John Angelillo
32-33: WORDS: Medium.com: Lais L, Elle.com: Alyssa Bailey, Dazed.com: Taylor Glasby, Instagram: @J-Hope 31 July 2022, RollingStoneIndia.com: Riddhi Chakraborty
PICTURES: Alamy Images, CJ Rivera/Everett Collection/Alamy Live News / Alamy Images, Rob Grabowski/Invision/AP / Alamy Images, Yonhap/Newcom/Alamy Live News / Alamy Images, Disney Media Distribution
34-35: WORDS: Vogue.com: Naomi Pike
PICTURES: Alamy Images, Matt Sayles/Invision/AP / YouTube, 'No More Dream' music video, 'I Need U' music video, 'Save Me' music video, 'Permission to Dance' music video, 'DNA' music video, 'Spring Day' music video, 'Black Swan' music video
36-37: WORDS: Refinery29.com: Natalie Morin
PICTURES: Alamy Images, Trafalgar Releasing / Courtesy Everett Collection / Alamy Images, Yonhap/Newcom/Alamy Live News / Alamy Images, Fathom Events / courtesy Everett Collection / Alamy Images, Imaginechina Limited
38-39: WORDS: Time.com: Raisa Burner, RollingStone.com: Brian Hiatt
PICTURES: Alamy Images, Tammie Arroyo/AFF-USA / Alamy Images, Pacific Press Media Production Corp / Alamy Images, MTV via Sipa USA / Alamy Images, Yonhap/Newcom/Alamy Live News, Alamy Images, OConnor / AFF-USA / Shutterstock
40-41: WORDS: Dazed.com: Taylor Glasby, Billboard.com: Tamar Herman, Teen Vogue.com: Taylor Glasby
PICTURES: Alamy Images, Aflo Co.Ltd/Nippon News / Alamy Images, CJ Rivera/Everett Collection/Alamy Live News / Alamy Images, Pictorial Press Ltd / Alamy Images, UPI/Alamy Live News / RCF/Everett Collection/Alamy Live News
42-43: WORDS: 'Outro: Tear': BTS, Billboard.com: E Alex Jung, Rolling Stone.com: Brian Hiatt
PICTURES: Alamy Images, Yonhap/Newcom/Alamy Live News
44-45: WORDS: Billboard.com: E Alex Jung
PICTURES: Alamy Images, Famous/ Bang Media International
YouTube, 'On' music video, 'Black Swan' music video, 'Mic Drop' music video, 'Boy with Luv' music video, 'Idol' music video
48-49: WORDS: Rolling Stone.com: Michelle Hyun Kim, Billboard.com: Starr Bowenbank
PICTURES: Alamy Images, Persona/Entertainment Pictures / Alamy Images, AP Photo/Andrew Harnik / Alamy Images, dpa/Alamy Live News, YouTube, 'Permission to Dance' music video
50-51: WORDS: Vogue.com: Taylor Glasby, *The Tonight Show Starring Jimmy Fallon:* Jimmy Fallon, 14 July 2021
PICTURES: Alamy Images, SOPA Images Limited/Alamy Live News / Alamy Images, Famous/Bang Media International
52-53: WORDS: Billboard.com: Hannah Dailey, Korea Herald.com: Choi Ji-won, UNICEF.org, *Burn The Stage*
PICTURES: Alamy Images, BJ Warnick/Newscom / Alamy Images, Lee Jin-wook/Yonhap via AP / Alamy Images, Trafalgar Releasing /Courtesy Everett Collection / Alamy Images
54-55: WORDS: NME.com: Gladys Yeo, Rolling Stone.com: Kat Bouza
PICTURES: Shutterstock, Rob Latour / Alamy Images, AP Photo/Chris Pizzello / Shutterstock, Emily Feary / Shutterstock, Sterling Munksgard / Shutterstock, Debby Wong / Shutterstock, Jamie Lamor Thompson
56-57: WORDS: SBS Star.net, BTS Japan Official Fanclub Magazine, Vol. 3, 9 November 2016
PICTURES: Alamy Images, BJ Warnick/Newscom / Alamy Images, Yonhap/Newcom/Alamy Live News / Alamy Images, Aflo Co.Ltd/Nippon News / Alamy Images, Newscom/Alamy Live News
58-59: WORDS: RollingStoneIndia.com: Riddhi Chakraborty, Billboard.com: Glenn Rowley, WeVerse Magazine, 1 July 2025
PICTURES: Alamy Images, AP Photo/Lee Jin-man / Alamy Images, AP Photo/Chris Pizzello
60-61: WORDS: Billboard.com: Gil Kaufman, Chosun News: Kang Dong Chu, Koreaboo.com: Danielle Song,
PICTURES: Alamy Images, AP Photo/Chris Pizzello / Alamy Images, Jordan Strauss/Invision/AP / Alamy Images, Matt Sayles/Invision/AP / Alamy Images, TopPhoto/Alamy Live News
62-63: WORDS: X.com, @rm_twt_official, 21 May 2017
PICTURES: Shutterstock, Kim Jae-Hwan/SOPA Images / Alamy Images, Nippon News/AFLO / Shutterstock, Rob Latour / Alamy Images, Chris Pizzello/Invision/AP / Shutterstock, Featureflash Photo Agency
64-65: WORDS: RollingStone.com: Brian Hiatt, Forbes.com: Hugh McIntyre, RollingStoneIndia.com: Riddhi Chakraborty, Mega-Asia.com: Jemma Cruz
PICTURES: Alamy Images, AP/AdamDavy / Alamy Images, Paul Frogratt / Shutterstock, Seokyong Lee/Penta Press / Alamy Images, Aflo Co.Ltd/Nippon News / Shutterstock, Silvia Elizabeth Pangaro
66-67: WORDS: Billboard.com: Gil Kaufman, Soompi.com: Clara Hong, Time.com: Halsey
PICTURES: Shutterstock, Speed Media / Alamy Images, AP Photo/Chris Pizzello, YouTube, 'Butter' music video / Shutterstock, Tinseltown
68-69: WORDS: Billboard.com: Heran Mamo
PICTURES: Shutterstock, Kim Hee-Chul/EPA / Shutterstock, KIM HEE-CHUL/EPA-EFE / Debora Himawan